Acclaim for *A View from My Window:
15 Sermons of Hope and Assurance* by A. Knighton Stanley

For over 40 years, Dr. Stanley's preaching has attempted to move a complex, sophisticated community beyond the "kindergarten" Christianity of its childhood to a powerful, relevant gospel that reconciles their complex lives while affirming the simple truth that in spite of all of our shortcomings, we are all God's beloved children. This volume illuminates a life and ministry obedient to a worthy call.

—Ambassador Andrew Young
Civil Rights leader/minister/humanitarian
Atlanta, Georgia

One Sunday morning, Dr. Stanley preached a sermon that so illuminated an aspect of my life's journey that I wrote one of my strongest musical compositions. On the Sunday after Coretta Scott King died, through his teaching and preaching he showed us a woman with a deep moving spirit and commitment to justice. I was able to cry again as we closed the service singing the spiritual "There Is a Balm in Gilead." I have continually found inspiration and hope in Dr. Stanley's words. May you also find water in your dry times from this well.

—Dr. Bernice Johnson Reagon
singer/composer/cultural historian
Washington, DC

This volume of sermons by Dr. A. Knighton Stanley is inspiring and instructive for laity and preachers alike. His evocative weaving of solid theological scholarship, illustrations from daily life, and his personal faith journey create a tapestry that compellingly presents the hope and joy of the good news. Taking a view from his window is to see the fullness of God's majesty.

—Rev. Dr. Henry T. Simmons
Senior Minister, St. Albans Congregational Church
St. Albans, New York

Dr. Stanley is passionate in his love for God and his service toward God's people. I so appreciate his openness and candor about his struggles as he continues to know and live the ways of God. This collection of sermons offers a glimpse into the life and soul of a preacher on his journey toward the heart of God.

—Rev. Natalie V. McLean, Chaplain
Bennett College for Women
Greensboro, North Carolina

A View from My Window is a refreshing, unassuming collection of a preacher's thoughts and reflections about God and who we are as God's children. Tony Stanley has a unique gift of sharing experiences of life through the lens of God's love, mercy, and faithfulness to all people. While reading his sermons, one feels as if one is reading over his shoulder as he journals about his life, ministry, and how God's love overshadows every nuance of what we do. Dr. Stanley has a gift of making the most mundane occurrence appear in reflection as a great epiphany in him. This book is a must-read for every preacher and especially seminarians.

—Rev. Dr. Susan D. Newman
Author, *Your Inner Eve: Discovering God's Woman Within*

A. Knighton Stanley's earlier book, The Children Is Crying (1979), addresses the American Missionary Association and the Congregational Church's blatant disregard for the rich and meaningful culture already existent among Afro Americans in the South following the Civil War and suggests that because of their failure to establish culturally relevant churches throughout the South, "The children, black and white, are crying every day." It is entirely providential, therefore, that this sensitive pastor/scholar/preacher now shares with us thought-provoking sermons that provide words of hope and encouragement so that we may cease our crying and more faithfully be the Body of Christ.

—Rev. Dr. Marvin L. Morgan
Moderator, General Synod 27
United Church of Christ

A Song at Midnight

A Song at Midnight

More Sermons of Hope and Assurance

A. Knighton Stanley

A Song at Midnight: More Sermons of Hope and Assurance

© 2020 The Family of A. Knighton Stanley

All rights reserved. No part of this book may be reproduced or transmitted in any form or by any means, electronic or mechanical, including photocopying, recording, or by any information storage and retrieval system, without permission in writing from the Publisher.

ISBN: 978-1-948638-10-4 (paperback)

Published by:
Fideli Publishing, Inc.
119 W Morgan St
Martinsville, IN 46151

www.FideliPublishing.com

Unless otherwise indicated, Bible quotations are from the New Revised Standard Version Bible, copyright © 1989 the Division of Christian Education of the National Council of the Churches of Christ in the United States of America. Used by permission. All rights reserved.

As indicated, Bible quotations are also from The Holy Bible, King James Version (KJV).

Contents

Preface ix
    by Rev. Brandon Harris

1. Empty-handed before God 1
2. Do the Right Thing! 11
3. Song at Midnight 21
4. The Decolonization of Matthew 31
5. Someone to Follow and a Place to Be 39
6. A Stumbling Savior 49
7. The Real Need of the Given to Give 57
8. One in the Spirit—One in the Lord 65
9. No More Walls 75
10. The Importance of Memory in Difficult Times 83
11. Having Church 95

In Memoriam

    Notes on Spirituality by A. Knighton Stanley,
        A Remembrance 107
        by Rev. George B. Walker Jr.
    Introduction to Funeral Sermon 113
        by Sushama Austin-Connor

12. Never Give Up (A Funeral Sermon) 117

    In Memoriam: A Memorial Poem for Tony 127
        by Lyvonne "Proverbs" Briggs

Afterword 131
    by Kathryn V. Stanley

About the Author 133

Preface
Rev. Brandon Harris

The King James Version of Romans 10:14 states: "How then shall they call on him in whom they have not believed? and how shall they believe in him of whom they have not heard? and how shall they hear without a preacher?"

In a post-modern society, where a plurality of voices in the public square is viewed as a challenge, and in a cultural and political moment where racial intolerance, bigotry, and divisiveness are championed, the words of the Rev. Dr. A. Knighton Stanley ring through time, challenging us to hear: Is there a word from the Lord? Is there a liberating, life-giving God who tears down the barriers that separate us from God and each other?

Rev. Dr. A. Knighton Stanley was a preacher who was willing to speak to the complexities of the Christian faith and the socio-political challenges of the day. Dr. Stanley's life and ministry embodied the best of the Black Congregationalist Tradition—a distinctive theological tradition uniting the freedom of conscience of the European congregational tradition with a passion for education and justice, anchored in an African spirituality that proclaimed the somebodiness of each human being. This faith was found in congregations such as Plymouth United Church of Christ, Detroit; First Congregational United Church of Christ, Atlanta; Dixwell Avenue Congregational Church, New Haven; and Peoples Congregational and Plymouth Congregational, Washington, D.C.

Dr. Stanley, anchored through six generations of the Black Congregationalist Tradition, proclaimed a liberating gospel that transformed the lives of those who heard his words. Dr. Stanley's sermons compel us to place our faith in a God who loves and sustains us while simultaneously putting those words into action so that the world might become a place where our "children might fly."

Dr. Stanley's life and legacy have encouraged me to fly in my own life. Though I never knew him, my life has been touched by his legacy. Though I was raised pentecostal and ordained American Baptist, my life has crossed with Dr. Stanley through the churches he loved and served. My great-aunt, a long-time member of the Plymouth Congregational Church of Detroit, often spoke of the young associate minister, Tony Stanley, who had served her beloved Church. I have had the blessing of being mentored by clergy whom Dr. Stanley himself had mentored including the Rev. Nicholas Hood, III and Dr. Dwight Andrews. Many Sundays when my own soul as a college chaplain needs renewal I find myself in the balcony or the back pews of the Peoples Congregational United Church of Christ in Washington D.C. There, as the music of the chancel choir floats over my head, I look at the windows of that great church and find myself renewed in the community of faith that Dr. Stanley led for over forty years.

Preface

Though I am not a United Church of Christ minister, I consider myself a spiritual son of the Rev. Dr. A. Knighton Stanley. In times of discouragement and joy I turn to his sermons and find myself renewed and challenged to believe again, to love again, and to serve a world so desperately in need of good news. You will find in this volume a word of hope that speaks through the ages.

Nota Bene: When I offered the preface to this book, little did I know that I would become the pastor of Peoples' Church in 2019. There are no coincidences in God's economy. I believe the experiences I had as a child at my aunt's church, reading Dr. Stanley's sermons, and allowing God's spirit to renew me from the balcony of the "African hut in cathedral proportions" have all prepared me to partner with God and Peoples' people to move us closer to the beloved community and to continue the work begun under the leadership of Rev. Dr. A. Knighton Stanley.

1

Empty-handed before God

When Jesus saw the crowds, he went up the mountain; and after he sat down, his disciples came to him. Then he began to speak, and taught them, saying:

"Blessed are the poor in spirit, for theirs is the kingdom of heaven.

"Blessed are those who mourn, for they will be comforted.

"Blessed are the meek, for they will inherit the earth.

"Blessed are those who hunger and thirst for righteousness, for they will be filled.

"Blessed are the merciful, for they will receive mercy.

"Blessed are the pure in heart, for they will see God.

"Blessed are the peacemakers, for they will be called children of God.

"Blessed are those who are persecuted for righteousness' sake, for theirs is the kingdom of heaven.

"Blessed are you when people revile you and persecute you and utter all kinds of evil against you falsely on my account."

(Matthew 5:1-11)

In the year 1946, I was 9 years old, and in fourth grade. That was a long time ago. Third grade had not been a great year. My class had been housed in a temporary barrack-looking building which was already 30-some years old by the time we occupied it. Even in the mid 1940s we as African American children knew that these buildings were inferior and were designed to make a statement about what the powers that were thought of us. Having endured a not-so-good year in third grade, I nonetheless felt ready for fourth grade, which was housed in a building 40 years old, but was at least made of brick and had convenient, indoor toilets.

I was determined that fourth grade would be better than third grade. So after attending school on opening day, and having been issued more books than I'd ever been issued before, I felt encouraged. I had a sense of being off to the academic races.

I knew from previous experience that getting to school on time was a virtue, devoutly to be followed, so on the second day of school I was not just on time, I got there early. Having a few minutes to spare before school "took in," as we used to say, the playground beckoned to me. After a few minutes, my playground time was interrupted by the first morning bell, at the sounding of which I skipped merrily and enthusiastically to my fourth-grade classroom for my second day. My fourth-grade teacher was a handsome woman who, even after I became an adult, looked larger than life. She stood just outside the door. Unintentionally, I'm sure, she intimidated us all as we entered her classroom.

As I passed, I gave her a big ingratiating smile, as only a fourth-grade boy can give, and said with a certain lyrical quality to my voice, "Good morning, Teacher." Appearing unimpressed, the teacher she said only, "Boy, where are your books?" Her unforgiving voice frightened me out of my wits and I managed very timidly to say, "I don't know where my books are. I suppose I left them on the playground." "Well," she said, "just suppose you march yourself back to the playground and find them."

I had no recourse but to accept her advice, so I marched myself back to the playground and searched high and low. But my books were nowhere to be found. Slowly I turned away from the playground, and at a snail's pace, as if in a funeral procession, marched myself back to the classroom. I managed to shed a tear or two as I entered the classroom hoping that crying a bit would give me a stay of execution. But alas, it did not work. When the teacher saw that I had returned with no books, she said, "You didn't find them, huh? Well then, you just march yourself down to the principal's office and you tell him you've lost your books on the second day of school." (From that day, it seemed that the teacher was always marching me somewhere. In fact, I spent the whole year being marched from here to there. I didn't learn much in her classroom, though I became an expert in marching.)

When I marched down to the principal's office, I came face to face with the greatly-to-be-feared-and-dreaded head of school. While the principal was not much taller than I was, he seemed awesome nonetheless. He spoke loudly and carried a small stick. When I tried to explain to him that his awful playground had mysteriously eaten my books, the principal would hear none of it. "Only the second day of school," he said with disdain, "and you've lost all your books. You are pitiful!!" he said. "I guess for the rest of this year you'll have to come to school without books—empty-headed, empty-handed—playing the fool." I felt as if I had been whittled down to nothing.

As if to dramatize my plight, the principal had me stand in a corner of his cluttered office, arms outstretched, hands opened wide so that I could look at my empty hands and be reminded that I had lost all of my books. I had nothing that was needed to be a good student in his school. Whenever I began to fidget and become unfocused, he would remind me with a decisive sternness, "Boy, don't you dare take your eyes off those empty hands. The very idea of you having lost your books!"

The experience of standing before that principal with no books, with empty hands, is an experience I can never forget. I've always been afraid that one day I might come up short before the powers that judge us in life and stand before them with hands empty, void of what the great judge values most. I came to believe that empty-handedness is a discomfort, a disease to be avoided at all cost.

But, isn't it true that from time to time all of us stand in the corners, in the shadows, on the margins of life before that which judges us, looking at our empty hands? There is a sense in which all of us are empty-handed. We live lives supplied with everything we really need. We may not have everything we want, but we have everything we need. Yet if we were to take all of these showers of material blessings away, and get right down to the bare bones, the real nitty-gritty of our humanity, we would find that something is missing at the very center of our lives. Somehow, in our human spirits, we stand naked—empty-handed before all of those things which seem to judge our lives. We have lost our sense of purpose, our sense of moral meaning. Rich, poor, young, old, black or white, somewhere in between, we all know what it means to be empty, to fail, to come up short, to be broken, to be weighed in the balance and found wanting. No matter how happy or successful we are, no matter how together we seem to be, down beneath all of our lives we are all the same. We live in the dull homes where something is missing. We live unfulfilled lives of empty-handedness. We struggle with the silence of unanswered prayer.

For down beneath and behind all that is good in the universe there is a world where people come up short, where people are looking for something, where people miss out on the sum and substance of life. Before whatever judges us in the world, we stand as I stood before my grade-school principal: empty-handed, afraid, ashamed, alone.

Yet there is a sense in which empty-handedness is not a bad thing. There is good news in our empty-handedness because, you see, there is a power before which we can stand empty-handed and we need neither be ashamed nor afraid. Indeed, there is a power before which empty-handedness is the only way to stand.

The late Henri J.M. Nouwen, a Catholic priest who taught at Yale Divinity School, in his book titled *With Open Hands,* speaks to the tension of tightly clenched fist as he tells the story of an elderly woman brought to a psychiatric hospital:

> She was wild, swinging at everything in sight, and frightening everyone so much that the doctors had to take everything away from her.

> But there was one small coin that she gripped in her fist and would not give up. In fact, it took two people to pry open that clenched hand. It was as though she would lose her very self along with the coin. If they deprived her of that last possession, she would have nothing more and be nothing more. That was her fear.[1]

So often, we, like this woman, go through life with clenched spirits, clenched fists, holding steadfast to worthless and meaningless things. We hold on to pride, emptiness, and arrogance. We seem to believe if we let these useless things go, we will lose our personhood, our integrity, our identity. So we hold on to that which represents nothing. But Father Nouwen says there is one before whom we need not bring our worthless possessions and clenched fists. There is one before whom we need not argue our cause. As we stand before God, we need only to open our clenched fists, to close our ceaselessly speaking mouths, and to stand empty-handed and closed-mouthed in the presence of God.[2]

God is the one before whom we can stand with closed mouths and nothing in our hands. Before we come, we need neither be afraid nor ashamed. In fact we must stand so in God's presence. For if we do not stand before God with empty hands, we will find ourselves unable to receive the blessed gift God gives. If we do not stand before God with our mouths closed and hearts open, we cannot hear what God has to say.

Years ago I was going through one horrific moment in life that we all seem to go through. Mid-life crisis, we call it today.

Empty-handed Before God

It was a moment of melancholy and depression. I couldn't eat or sleep, so I got up early one morning. I sat at my kitchen table crying in my coffee, trying to find the way. I found myself talking aloud to God. I found myself telling God what God had to do to straighten out my life. I told God, "God, this is my agenda. This is the way my life needs to work. God, get busy and do what I'm telling you to do." For several days, I got up early in the morning and had these deep talks with God. I brought my hands and head and heart filled with things God needed to change and do for me.

Despite this new routine, none of this was working for me. I was insistent upon ordering God to sit up and beg, but God refused to sit up and beg. One morning when I was at my wits end and I ceased asking, "God, what is the matter with you?" instead, I said, "God, what is the matter with *me*? Was my father a better man than I? He always seemed so wise—always knew what to say and do to pull his life together and move on down the road. When he stood before you, God, you always seemed to answer. I wish I knew what I was doing like he did."

But then it occurred to me that my father didn't know what he was doing either. The difference was this: he knew that he didn't know. So when he came to the table with God, he came, as we say in the Lord's Supper liturgy, "not to express an opinion, but to pray for a spirit." He didn't come with an agenda. He came with an open heart. He didn't come with a mouthful of advice for God. He came in simple trust and quiet humility. He did not come with his fists clenched with what was worthless and meaningless. Rather, he came with empty hands and an open heart, hungering and thirsting for a word from the Lord.

My father had other virtues which revealed God to him. My father loved to garden; he was good at it. But as I watched him garden for many years, I came to realize that fruits and vegetables were not the ultimate harvest from his gardening experience. At sunrise, he would go to his garden, not simply to plant, water, and weed, but he would go there to commune with God, to have a little talk with Jesus so that his spirit and life would be made right. That was the real harvest. My father was a gentle but strong spirit, who, in his garden, stood before God as an empty pitcher before a full fountain. He always came out of his garden with a blessing and word from the Lord. That was the real harvest.

So often in our meeting with God we come away with no word, no blessing, no nothing, not because we come before God with too little, but because we come before God with too much.

Isn't it interesting that according to Matthew 5, the first words out of the mouth of Jesus in his first sermon are these: "Blessed are the poor in spirit"? In other words, blessed are the empty-handed ones; blessed are the ones who come up short. Blessed are those who recognize their need and stand without pretense before God. Blessed are those who have reached rock bottom, those who know that they cannot live without the help of God. Blessed are those who come just as they are without a word, without one plea.

You can trust the extravagance of God. You don't need to bring anything to God's table. For God's table is not a potluck;

it's a banquet, a feast. So come. But when you come, come not to express an opinion, but to seek a presence and to encounter the Spirit. Come with nothing and be blessed. Blessed are they who come with nothing, for they shall leave God's table of extravagant abundance with every good thing they need.

Dear God, empty-handed I stand before you. All I need is a hunger to be blessed by you. Bless me even now, dear God.
Bless me even now.
Amen.

Notes

1. Henri J.M. Nouwen, *With Open Hands* (Notre Dame, IN: Ave Maria Press, 2006), 20.
2. Ibid., 19–27.

2

Do the Right Thing!

The apostles said to the Lord, "Increase our faith!" The Lord replied, "If you had faith the size of a mustard seed, you could say to this mulberry tree, 'Be uprooted and planted in the sea,' and it would obey you.

"Who among you would say to your slave who has just come in from plowing or tending sheep in the field, 'Come here at once and take your place at the table'? Would you not rather say to him, 'Prepare supper for me, put on your apron and serve me while I eat and drink; later you may eat and drink'? Do you thank the slave for doing what was commanded? So you also, when you have done all that you were ordered to do, say, 'We are worthless slaves; we have done only what we ought to have done!'"

(Luke 17:5-10)

History amply illustrates that language is not static. Rather, language is fluid. It is a dynamic reality which is forever in a state of flux and change. Consider this illustration: upon his completion of London's St. Paul's Cathedral, Sir Christopher Wren was obliged, upon Queen Anne's request, to take her on a tour of his monumental work. It is said that after the Queen had completed the tour she described it as "awful, artificial, and amusing." In our day if we described someone's monumental work as "awful, artificial, and amusing," he or she would be duly offended. But in the 18th Century when Queen Anne responded to Sir Christopher's brilliant architectural achievement with these words, he was greatly complimented because "awful" meant awe-inspiring, "artificial" meant "artistic," and amusing meant "amazing." When Queen Anne called St. Paul's Cathedral "awful, artificial, and amusing" she was calling it "awe-inspiring, artistic, and "amazing."

Historically, language is not set in concrete. Language is a product of its culture, a child of its time. This means then that if we are not a part of the age, culture, or place out of which a particular expression comes we may have difficulty understanding it.

The same is true of some of the words and expressions of Jesus. The people of Jesus' time seemed to realize that truth comes in a variety of linguistic forms. Truth as fact is only one of those forms. For example in Luke 17:5-10, when Jesus speaks of a faith that can uproot a mulberry tree, he conveys a symbolic truth. He is saying that if one opens oneself to a faith which comes from a relationship of trust in God, then one will begin to recognize unique power. Jesus is saying that great potency comes to those who put their trust in him. Jesus is saying to the Apostles, "You can do all things in the God you trust, who gives you plenty." When Jesus says to the Apostles, "If you had faith no bigger than a mustard seed, you could say to this mulberry tree, be uprooted and replanted in the sea, and it would obey you," Jesus is not giving us a statement or description of fact. Nonetheless, you can bet your life that Jesus is speaking the truth.

Language is not static. Language is always in a state of flux and change. Language is a child of its time, its culture, and its place.

In the second part of today's Gospel lesson, Jesus tells a parable about a slave who was both a house slave and a field hand. Jesus makes it clear that the slave fully obeys the rules of slavery. When he comes in from the fields, he doesn't sit down and serve himself an abundant meal; rather, he serves his master. Even without thanks, he serves his master because it is his duty to do so.

The story about the dutiful slave offends our 21st-century sensibilities, but let us be clear that Jesus is not telling this parable to affirm the rightness of the institution of slavery. Although Christian slave traders of the 16th, 17th, and 18th centuries used this passage to justify the "peculiar institution," Jesus, in this parable, is bringing to bear the language of his time, his culture, and his place. When Jesus tells the parable of the slave and the master, he is speaking beyond the boundaries of space and time, and his audience knew this. Jesus is saying that all human beings—regardless of their circumstances in life—have a responsibility to exceed their life's station and boundaries and do the right thing in keeping with the will of God. Jesus uses this parable to say that even if you are born into slavery—as evil and harsh as slavery is—you have a God-given imperative to live beyond the confines of your "slaveness" and be the best that you can be.

All of us love to give excuses for why we can't do one thing or another. We are too old, too young, too rich, too poor, too black, too white, too whatever. We give a dozen excuses as to why we can't get on with the business of life. These verses from Luke 17 challenge us to live beyond the excuses and limitations. By God's grace, we have to do the right thing and give life all we've got.

I've known so many, many people who have done just that. For example, I've seen school children in Africa who had everything going against them. Some were orphans. Many walked long miles to go to school, and they were hungry or severely malnourished. Others had serious birth defects. Their makeshift classrooms were made from abandoned cargo crates or straw. Their teachers often had only a high school diploma, if that. Their teachers taught as many as 80 pupils of 4 different grades in one hot classroom. These African students usually had no pencil, paper, or books of their own. They were taught despite circumstances under which the educational experts say that students are not capable of learning. And yet, I've seen African students graduate from what we would regarded as horrible, impossible schools and be able to compete with the very best minds in the world.

In a modern world of plenty and abundance it is shameful, sinful even, that these African children must be educated under such circumstances.

At the same time that we work to improve the awful circumstances under which African children are educated, we must applaud and encourage those who live beyond the circumstances and constrictions of an extremely harsh environment and become the best they can be and who ably compete in the marketplaces of the world.

Because of their circumstances, the average child in the central cities of urban America could be representative of all the sophisticated psychological, sociological, and political reasons that they are not supposed to learn. Make no mistake about it, the awful circumstances which even some of these children describe are not all excuses; they are real. But even as we seek to address and correct these harsh social and political realities under which we must rear and educate our children, we must encourage our children to press the envelope and do what many of their forebears did—to live beyond their circumstances, to do the right thing, and to break out of what the world expects of them and be the best that they can be.

On May 17, 1954, when I was a junior in high school, the United States Supreme Court handed down its landmark decision in *Brown v. Board of Education* of Topeka, Kansas, in which the Court declared state laws establishing separate public schools for black and white students to be unconstitutional because state laws requiring "separate but equal" schools violated the Equal Protection Clause of the Fourteenth Amendment. Ostensibly, this decision struck down *Plessy v. Ferguson*, the U.S. Supreme Court's 1896 decision that upheld the constitutionality of racial segregation laws for public facilities as long as the segregated facilities were equal in quality, a doctrine that came to be known as "separate but equal." Yet 60 years after *Brown*, and 110 years after *Plessy*, we still remain separate and, by and large, unequal.

On the fiftieth anniversary of that historic *Brown* decision, I sat with those who were planning marches and celebrations in the Nation's Capital marking the historic event. The plan included a rally in front of the Supreme Court building to remind the nation of the unfinished business of 1954. For the most part, the marchers were college and high school students. When we discussed from what point the march to the Supreme Court should originate, I suggested that it should originate from the U.S. Department of Education. It should start in front of the United States Department of Education with students indicting this nation for not delivering the quality and excellence in public education promised in *Brown*. But it shouldn't stop there, I offered. The students needed to indict the mayor, the council, and the school board because they too had fumbled the ball and had done little to advance the promise of excellence in *Brown*. They've not done the right thing by our children.

In urban areas all over the nation, even today, we seem helpless to prepare our children to be the best they can be.

Several years ago, I presided over the welcoming ceremony for the replica of the slave ship Amistad in the Baltimore Harbor. As I sat on the shores of the Chesapeake Bay, I was reminded that Mr. Frederick Douglass worked and played around the Baltimore Harbor when he was a boy. Mr. Douglass, as you remember, was born a slave. As a young slave boy, he was sent by his master to live with his master's relatives in Baltimore because Frederick was incorrigible as a slave. The master's wife, Mrs. Auld, started teaching the young Frederick the alphabet because she was bored and had little else to do. One day the master came home unexpectedly and found his wife teaching young Frederick to read. Flabbergasted, he pulled his wife aside and forbade her to teach Frederick to read. He said to her, "If you teach that boy how to read, or educate him, then he can never be a slave again."

Frederick heard these words and decided that an educated gentleman—a free man—was what he wanted to be. Frederick decided to steal bread from his master's table, take it to the streets of Baltimore, and give it to poor white children who were educated in the free schools of Baltimore in exchange for help with reading. This is how he learned to read. As a young man, as a ship-builder helper, Mr. Douglass began his education in the Baltimore Harbor because he learned letters, numbers, and words as he helped put together parts of the ships. He studied the labels on the ship parts. As he studied the labels, he learned to read but he also came to understand, even more fully than his master, that if you educate a person and remove the veil of ignorance from their eyes he or she can never be a slave again. Mr. Douglass decided that he would live beyond the constrictions of his "slaveness." He would honor his "Child of God-ness," do the right thing, and be the best he could be.

Martin Luther King Jr. said, "Whatever your life's work is, never consider it insignificant. If it is for the uplifting of humanity, it has cosmic significance, however small it is. If you are called to a little job, seek to do it in a big way. If your life's work is confined to the ordinary, seek to do it in an extraordinary way. If you discover that you are called to be a street sweeper, sweep streets like Michelangelo painted pictures, like Beethoven composed music, and like Shakespeare wrote poetry. Sweep streets so well that all the host of heaven and earth will have to pause and say, 'Here lived a great street sweeper who [did] his job well.'"[1]

We always look for excuses not to live up to our Child of God-ness. We fail to reach beyond our human limitations. We fail to hold fast to our visions and dreams. In the parable before us, Jesus is not condoning slavery or inhumane servitude. Rather, in the language of his day, Jesus is saying that no matter what the world does to you, no matter how the world labels you, you are not slaves—excuse makers—you are not second-class citizens, you are God's colony in man's world. "Beloved," Jesus is saying, "you are the children of God." Though the world may treat you as a slave, a nobody, you must never let slave-ness overtake your Child of God-ness.

In all good things, press the envelope—live beyond your limitations and restrictions. Trust God, do the right thing, and be the best you can be. For if you trust God, if you have the faith of a mustard seed, you can say to a mulberry tree, "Be uprooted and be planted in the sea," and it will obey you. If you live beyond your human reaches by trusting in God, you can say to whatever mountain stands in your way, "Mountain be moved," and by God's grace the mountain will move.

> *God of Grace and God of Glory,*
> *on your people pour your power.*
> *We feel so weak, so inadequate sometimes,*
> *but as people of little, help us remember*
> *that you never give us a task*
> *without providing the strength for its fulfillment.*

*By your grace, give us power to do your holy will.
Give us moral muscle to remove mountains of despair, and to
exalt valleys of apathy, weak self-confidence, and resignation.
Let us know it is not what's done to us that really matters,
it is what we do with what is done to us which really counts.
In our trials, let Jesus walk with us.
And when we are blinded by the burdens of life,
open our eyes that we may see.
Amen.*

Note

1. Martin Luther King Jr., "Three Dimensions of a Complete Life," draft, www.thekingcenter.org/archive/document/three-dimensions-complete-life (accessed February 27, 2018).

3

Song at Midnight

One day, as we were going to the place of prayer, we met a slave-girl who had a spirit of divination and brought her owners a great deal of money by fortune-telling. While she followed Paul and us, she would cry out, "These men are slaves of the Most High God, who proclaim to you a way of salvation." She kept doing this for many days. But Paul, very much annoyed, turned and said to the spirit, "I order you in the name of Jesus Christ to come out of her." And it came out that very hour.

But when her owners saw that their hope of making money was gone, they seized Paul and Silas and dragged them into the marketplace before the authorities. When they had brought them before the magistrates, they said, "These men are disturbing our city; they are Jews and are advocating customs that are not lawful for us as Romans to adopt or observe." The crowd joined in attacking them, and the magistrates had them stripped of their clothing and ordered them to be beaten with rods. After they had given them a severe flogging, they threw them into prison and ordered the jailer to keep them securely. Following these instructions, he put them in the innermost cell and fastened their feet in the stocks.

About midnight Paul and Silas were praying and singing hymns to God, and the prisoners were listening to them.

> *Suddenly there was an earthquake, so violent that the foundations of the prison were shaken; and immediately all the doors were opened and everyone's chains were unfastened. When the jailer woke up and saw the prison doors wide open, he drew his sword and was about to kill himself, since he supposed that the prisoners had escaped. But Paul shouted in a loud voice, "Do not harm yourself, for we are all here." The jailer called for lights, and rushing in, he fell down trembling before Paul and Silas. Then he brought them outside and said, "Sirs, what must I do to be saved?" They answered, "Believe on the Lord Jesus, and you will be saved, you and your household." They spoke the word of the Lord to him and to all who were in his house. At the same hour of the night he took them and washed their wounds; then he and his entire family were baptized without delay. He brought them up into the house and set food before them; and he and his entire household rejoiced that he had become a believer in God.*
>
> (Acts 16:16-34)

As I reflect on this passage, three images flood my imaginations. The first image is the children's book *The Little Engine That Could*.[1] When I was a child, I loved that story. As a child, I recall trying to learn new life skills and searching for new possibilities. I was inspired to greater heights by *The Little Engine That Could*. Even now, I hear the resilient voice of that little locomotive straining to get up the next steep hill, huffing and puffing and blaring as it goes, chanting as it strained, "I think I can! I think I can! I think I can!"

The second image takes me back to my early teen years when, having climbed Crowders Mountain, near Kings Mountain, North Carolina, I saw a tree growing out of a solid rock. It wasn't much of a tree; it was just a sapling. But I thought of how courageous that little tree was to defy nature. I thought of the courage it took to grow against all expectations out of a solid rock—huffing and puffing, chanting like the little locomotive, "I think I can! I think I can! I think I can!"

The third image is not unlike the first two. It is not my image but the image of the British poet Alfred Lord Tennyson. One day as Mr. Tennyson was walking in his neighborhood in London, he was struck by the persistence of a beautiful flower which grew, not out of rich soil, but out of a crack in a stone wall. So struck was he by the resilience of this flower, which courageously grew against the odds, that he memorialized his impression of it in a poem titled "Flower in the Crannied Wall." Alfred Lord Tennyson wrote:

> Flower in the crannied wall,
> I pluck you out of the crannies,
> I hold you here, root and all, in my hand,
> Little flower—but if I could understand
> What you are, root and all, and all in all,
> I should know what God and man is.[2]

That is deep, isn't it? Alfred Lord Tennyson says if he can understand what made that flower grow—if he could understand what courage and persistence caused that flower to keep on keeping on, defying nature and growing out of a crack in a stone wall, if only he could understand what motivated this flower to persist, he would understand the greatest mysteries of the universe and of the human life; he would know what man is and what God is.

So we have them, these three images: the little train, which even against the odds thought it could; a tree which stubbornly grows out of a solid rock; and a flower which mysteriously grows out of the crack in the stone wall shedding light on life's deepest mysteries.

As I think of the train, the tree, and the flower, I gaze in wonder to their witness of the resilience of life. Just as the powerful images of the train, the tree, and the flower flood my memory, so too does the image of Paul and Silas in Acts 16:16-34. The picture painted in this passage of Scripture is that of two followers of Jesus being cast in prison after exorcising a demon from a slave girl.

After being stripped, beaten, and flogged; after having their feet placed in chains, it would seem that the brutality of it all would have silenced their witness to faith and hope and would have blunted the resilience of the life they shared in Jesus Christ. But not so. Instead of giving up, their faith proved to be as stubborn as the little train huffing and puffing its way up a steep hill. Their faith seemed to be as persistent as a robust tree growing out of a solid rock. Their faith proved to be as tenacious as a flower peeking its head out of a crack in a stone wall.

The Scripture says that as Paul and Silas sat in prison in shackles, bound in chains, they didn't give up or give out. Nor did they cry the blues. Rather the Scripture says that, at about midnight, they were praying and singing hymns to God, even as they sat behind prison bars.

If we could understand just a little bit of what motivated Paul and Silas; if we could understand something of what made them keep the faith; if we could understand what, even in the face of such adversity, kept them singing, what kept them praying, even in the midnight hour of life; if we would understand a little better the mystery of the universe and human life; if we could understand what made Paul and Silas raise a hymn and lift a prayer in the middle of their darkest hour, then we would understand a little better what God and humankind are. Not only that, if we could know what made Paul and Silas keep on praying and singing even in the midnight hour, then we would understand something more of the irrepressible hope of the Gospel of Jesus Christ.

A train which thought it could, a tree growing out of a stone rock, a flower peeking out of a crack in a stone wall, and Paul and Silas singing in jail all bear witness to the resilience of life.

But these images do not stand alone. There is a sense in which the Civil Rights Movement of the 1960s also bore witness to the resilience of life and to the resilience of the life we have in Jesus Christ. The Civil Rights Movement of the 1960s was a religious revival, not unlike the First and Second Great Awakenings of another time.

It is fashionable in this day and time to say that matters of race in America are worse now than they were before *Brown v. Board of Education* and the Civil Rights Movement. When I hear otherwise intelligent people make this statement, I think that these people either were not living before the '60s or that they have lost their memories if not their minds. That is pure lunacy. Things are far better now than they were before *Brown v. Board* and the Civil Rights Movement. The goals of *Brown* and the struggles of the Civil Rights Movement were as audacious as the little weighted-down, under-steamed train trying to get up a steep hill. The struggle of the Civil Rights Movement was as uncanny as trees growing out of a rock. The nonviolent methodology and strategy of the Civil Rights Movement was as courageous and irrational as a flower emerging out of a stone wall. It was as religious as Paul and Silas praying and singing in jail.

It is certainly true of the Civil Rights Movement that had it not been for its religious fervor, had it not been that the Civil Rights Movement was an act of worship and faith, those who say we are worse off now than we were before would be absolutely right. The Civil Rights Movement in almost all of its parts was a religious revival. Those who were a part the movement believed in the hope of the Gospel even when they went to jail. They took the name of Jesus with them. They not only held on to each other but they held to God's unchanging hand in everything they said and did. The Civil Rights Movement was successful because, at its best, it was a revival of religion, a spiritual awakening, a moral rearmament. It clung to the very best of the faith. It called attention to the resilience of life and the tenacity of the life we share in Jesus Christ.

The late James Farmer used to love to tell the story of his having been arrested and jailed with a group of students of the movement in McComb, Mississippi. Mr. Farmer said it was cold and damp in that Mississippi jail. There were not enough cots to go around, but each of these political prisoners was given a thin, dirty blanket which provided their only protection from the cold and dampness of the jail's floor. Mr. Farmer said when night fell on that Mississippi jail, they were cold and a certain sadness and despair seemed to overcome them all. Then round about midnight, one of the students prayed a heartfelt prayer and lifted the hymn, "What a Friend We Have in Jesus." After that, another student raised one of the great songs of the movement, "Ain't Gonna Let Nobody Turn Me Around." Then another student led them in a spiritual saying, "Steal Away, Steal Away, Steal Away to Jesus."

Mr. Farmer said after the spiritual was sung, they heard the footsteps of the jail keeper moving in their direction of the cell. A silence fell upon them as they were deathly afraid of what the jail keeper might do. When the jail keeper got to the cell, he cussed them, calling them by the usual names, and told them that if they sang one more song he would take their blankets away. Mr. Farmer said the silence in that dark cold cell was so thick you could almost cut it. The thought of giving up those blankets in the cold of the night was more than they could bear. But then, as the jailer started back to his station, the silence was broken when one of the students shouted at the top of his voice: "Mr. Jail Keeper, you can take away our blankets, but you can't take away our spirits; you can't destroy our souls." With that, another student led them all in singing "I'm so glad Jesus lifted me, singing Glory Hallelujah, Jesus lifted me."

Even after their blankets were taken away, they sang hymns and freedom songs and prayed all night long. The bodies of these freedom fighters were cold, but their spirits were on fire. Since the movement was a spiritual awakening, they knew something of the irrepressible hope of the Gospel of Jesus Christ. Their souls were anchored in the Lord.

Shame on those who say we've made no progress. How little they know! Even if we do have a long way to go, we've come a long way from where we were. We have come this far by faith leaning on the Lord. Like modern-day Paul and Silas, we have been able to sing and pray even in the midnight hour, sometimes sacrificing our blankets and worldly goods, to save America's soul. On freedom's journey we have given witness to the resilience of life and the courage and hope that we share through life in Jesus Christ.

When I was involved in youth ministry years ago, we sang a lot. One of the songs we taught the young people was "Gimme That Ole Time Religion, It's Good Enough for Me." It was such a great song, after we sang give me old-time religion, we sang the next stanza, "It was good for my dear mother, my dear father, it's good enough for me." Then we'd sing, "It was good enough for Paul and Silas, it's good enough for me." When we were almost to the end, we'd sing, "It's good when the world's on fire, it's good enough for me."

Well, Friends, the world is on fire, the best I can tell. Fires are burning everywhere you look—in Egypt, Afghanistan, Iran, Iraq, New York—the smoke clouds are rising. In some parts of the world, some of our enlisted men and women seem to have gone berserk and higher-ups who hide behind medals, badges, rank, and titles have become chronic liars and cowards. Our peace-keeping forces have become perpetuators of brutality and indecency. They are the source of un-peace and unrest. Our president's best-laid plans have run amok and the leaders of our nation have lost its sense of moral meaning.

The smoke clouds are rising. The world *is* on fire and we need that ole-time religion, the religion of Paul and Silas, that's good enough for me. The faith of Paul and Silas was not an attitude of annoyance; theirs was not a faith that whistled in the dark. Theirs was a faith which prayed and sang hymns in the midnight hour; a faith which could face death, that could suffer prison and the lion's den. Why? Paul and Silas were able to sing and pray at midnight because they knew of the irrepressible hope of the Gospel of Jesus Christ. And because of this faith their lives give witness to the resilience of life, and especially to the life we have in Jesus Christ.

So we have, then, the little train that could, a tree growing out of a solid rock, a flower flourishing in a crack in a stone wall, students who understood that even coldness and jail cells do not a prison of the spirit make. Finally, there are Paul and Silas praying and singing so hard in prison at midnight that the walls shook and their chains came off.

If we can began to understand something of the persistent stubbornness of all these things, then we will begin to know of the mystery of the universe and the mystery of human life. If we can begin to understand these things, we may begin to understand who we are and who God is. If we have the courage and faith of these things, we may just have the ole-time religion, a saving faith. And, why not? It was good for me, my dear mother, my brother, for Ted Taylor and Ashton Thomas,[3] for Paul and Silas. Yes, it's good when the world's on fire, and it's good enough for me.

*Dear God, when the world is on fire,
when midnight comes into our lives,
give us a song that can shake open the prisons of our hearts
and draw us to life in Jesus Christ.
Amen.*

Notes

1. Watty Piper, *The Little Engine That Could* (New York: Grosset and Dunlap, 1978).

2. Alfred Lord Tennyson, "Flower in the Crannied Wall."

3. Ted Taylor and Ashton Thomas were faithful members of the author's congregation for many years. Both preceded him in death.

4

The Decolonization of Matthew

As Jesus was walking along, he saw a man called Matthew sitting at the tax booth; and he said to him, "Follow me." And he got up and followed him.

And as he sat at dinner in the house, many tax collectors and sinners came and were sitting with him and his disciples. When the Pharisees saw this, they said to his disciples, "Why does your teacher eat with tax collectors and sinners?" But when he heard this, he said, "Those who are well have no need of a physician, but those who are sick. Go and learn what this means, 'I desire mercy, not sacrifice.' For I have come to call not the righteous but sinners."

. . .

While he was saying these things to them, suddenly a leader of the synagogue came in and knelt before him, saying, "My daughter has just died; but come and lay your hand on her, and she will live." And Jesus got up and followed him, with his disciples. Then suddenly a woman who had been suffering from hemorrhages for twelve years came up behind him and touched the fringe of his cloak, for she said to herself, "If I only touch his cloak, I will be made well." Jesus turned, and seeing her he said, "Take heart, daughter; your faith has made you well." And instantly the woman was made well.

When Jesus came to the leader's house and saw the flute players and the crowd making a commotion, he said, "Go away; for the girl is not dead but sleeping." And they laughed at him. But when the crowd had been put outside, he went in and took her by the hand, and the girl got up. And the report of this spread throughout that district.

(Matthew 9:9-13, 18-26)

The Gospel lesson today is, at least in part, about the call of one whose name was Matthew. Matthew was a tax collector for the Roman Empire. Palestine was a colony of Rome. Matthew had been appointed by Rome to collect taxes from Palestinian Jews, whose homeland Rome had occupied and colonized. Matthew looked like a Palestinian Jew; Matthew spoke like a Palestinian Jew; and by blood and ancestor, he was a Palestinian Jew. But he had sold his soul to the company store. As a tax collector, Matthew was a collaborator, a representative of the oppressive Roman colonial power. All of the Palestinian Jews had been politically colonized by Rome.

Matthew was a victim of the most vicious colonization of them all. His was not simply a political colonization; his was an existential colonization. Rome had taken him over completely and colonized him, lock, stock, and barrel, spirit, mind, and soul. Rome had domesticated him by throwing him a bone. Rome had bought him out so completely that he was caught in a web woven of sin, money, career advancement, self-aggrandizement, deceit, and lies from which he could not extricate himself. So, although Matthew looked like a Palestinian

The Decolonization of Matthew

Jew, talked with the accent of a Palestinian Jew, and had the blood of a Palestinian Jew, when one visited his desk in the tax office one discovered that Matthew was an oppressive Roman colonizer through and through.

Matthew suffered the worst kind of colonization. His was the colonization of the mind. Although he worked for the empire, he was not free. Having said something religious and biblical, let me move on and bring this discussion close to home.

History amply illustrates that so very often when the formerly oppressed are given some semblance of freedom and power, they become as oppressive as those who formerly ruled over them. When I had the opportunity to meet the First Lady of Liberia, I was painfully reminded that under President Monroe, when African slaves in America were sent back to Africa to form a colony on the continent, they became as oppressive to the native settlers they found on the land as their slave masters had been to them. Nearly 150 years later, Liberia still sheds blood.

The formerly oppressed became, in fact, the oppressors. It is almost always the case that when the formerly oppressed are given some semblance of freedom and power, they are prone to become as oppressive as their masters were to them.

When we lived on Emerson Street in Washington, D.C., we had a neighbor named Mr. Hill. I never knew his first name. Mr. Hill was an older man, well in his 80's. He wore rubber boots up to his hips, a felt hat, overall, and a wool suit coat year-round. Mr. Hill was helpful to everyone in the neighborhood. He was so helpful and officious that we called the "Mayor of Emerson Street." Mr. Hill, I discovered was also a philosopher and political analyst of sorts. One day, in his home-spun way, Mr. Hill came to me and said "Rev., let me ask you a question. I've noticed that no matter what color the mayor is, they don't collect my trash over here (meaning in a black neighborhood) as good as they collect the trash over there (meaning in a white neighborhood). Rev.," he said, "why do you think that is?" After a brief pause, we both shrugged our shoulders pretending to be dumbfounded. But we knew, we both knew.

Mr. Hill continued, "Rev., I have another question for you. I've noticed that no matter what the color of the people who sit on the school board, the schools seem to educate the children over there (meaning in an affluent white neighborhood) better than they do over here (meaning in a poor black neighborhood). Rev.," he said, "why you think that is?" We both paused for a moment then shrugged our shoulders, pretending to be dumbfounded. Mr. Hill walked away, shaking his head as if in bewilderment. But we knew, we both knew.

So often, unbeknownst to and unintended by them, those who were formerly powerless who are given some semblance of power can become as oppressive as those who exerted oppressive power over them. The mayor and the chair of the school board had fallen prey to the colonization fallacy.

The mayor and the superintendent can be blacker than a thousand midnights, but the trains and the schools and trucks seem to run a little better over there than they do over here. I've sat on and with trustee boards and boards of governors, the members of which were accused of being incorrigible

The Decolonization of Matthew

tyrants, but low and behold when the accusers rose to memberships on those boards they were often more tyrannical than the tyrants who preceded them.

We have here a dilemma, don't we? How do we end this vicious cycle of tyranny and oppression in which we find ourselves?

The call of Matthew suggests a simple way out of this complicated cycle. The Gospel lesson says that while Matthew was sitting at his desk at the Roman tax office, Jesus came along one day and said, "Follow me." Without argument, without hesitation, without reservation, Matthew got up from his little Roman tax collector's desk and followed Jesus. It was as simple and as uncomplicated as that.

Now Jesus was not merely calling Matthew to follow him—as important as that was. Jesus was calling Matthew out of the mess he was in. He was calling Matthew out of the hands of Roman bondage, out of the bonds of money and superficial power. Jesus was calling Matthew to start a new life, a new way of being. Jesus was calling Matthew to be redeemed, liberated, saved, to be set free from every principality and power which enslaved and colonized his spirit and mind. Jesus was calling Matthew to let go of his old ways and to take up the Jesus way of being in the world. In the simple words "Follow me," Jesus was calling Matthew to embrace a new authority, a new set of values, and a new set of rules. Jesus called Matthew to saddle up and move out beyond the squalor of oppressive Roman power. Jesus called him to move out even beyond the legalism of his religious experience, to embrace a new set of religious values and pledge allegiance to an alternative realm.

In asking Matthew to follow him, Jesus invited Matthew to live in the present age based on the values of the Kingdom of God. Jesus called Matthew to establish God's colony in man's world. In calling Matthew out from an oppressive state and a legalistic religion, Jesus broke the vicious cycle of oppression so that Matthew could live a Kingdom life, unsold, unbought, liberated and free.

My wife once told me, when she was somewhere between a fit of affection and anger, "Tony, you are the most eccentric person I've ever met!" I was a little more than offended and baffled at being accused of being eccentric until I went to the dictionary and looked up the word eccentric actually means. I discovered that eccentric essentially means to stand outside of the circle. I said to myself, "Being eccentric, to stand outside the circle, to live and think outside the box, is the best thing that could have ever happened to me. To live outside of the clutches of all of these negative claims on my life makes me who I am and sets me free. If that is what eccentric is, then eccentric I shall be."

Mr. Frederick Douglass once said that in terms of racial and cultural and political orientation he was neither black nor white, rich nor poor. Rather he always aimed to speak, feel, believe, and hear as one who stands outside of the circle. Mr. Douglass was eccentric!

Eccentric is what Jesus called Matthew and us to be! When Jesus calls us to follow him, we are called to move outside the circle of the way things are to the way things ought to be. Jesus calls us to follow him beyond the circle of sin—and greed and money and career and race and deceit and gender and lies—

The Decolonization of Matthew

and to live with him even in the present age and place on the basis of the values of the Kingdom of God. Jesus invites us one and all to be eccentric and to live in this present age as if the reign of God has come.

My younger daughter, Taylor, went to a very fine school where racially she is a minority. Around the dinner table one Sunday, we discussed the challenges of trying to maintain balance in a place where one is in the minority. Taylor said that when she does some things which are culturally black her white friends tease her about being "ghetto," and when she speaks standard English with a crisp accent some of her black friends accuse her of being "white." She is damned if she does and damned if she doesn't. I asked Taylor with concern how she was able to deal with all of that, and without a pause she said, "Just fine. Culturally, I am neither black nor white nor Asian, but at best I am all and none of these. I am who I am and I feel good about that," she said, praise the Lord! Taylor is the kind of kid Martin King dreamed about! I then told Taylor no matter how lonely it becomes, always live outside the circle and think and be outside the box because that is where God and authentic life call us to be.

Jesus calls us to be eccentric, to live beyond all of the negative claims of this world, to think and speak and have our being outside the circle, to think and act and proclaim that Gospel, the good news of Jesus outside the box of what is. Jesus calls us to live in this present time and place as if we lived on the basis of the Kingdom of God. If we can live our lives as if in the Kingdom we can live beyond those values which bruise all nature and breach community. After all, that is what Jesus died for and that is what Jesus died about. That is where we should be and what we should be about if we have really heard Christ's call to be Christians and to follow him.

> *Dear God, your Son, Jesus was crucified*
> *outside the walls of Jerusalem.*
> *Give us the grace to stand outside the circle*
> *and to be who we are.*
> *We do not belong to this world;*
> *we are citizens of your Kingdom.*
> *Give us the courage to act like it.*
> *Amen.*

5

Someone to Follow and a Place to Be

The next day he saw Jesus coming toward him and declared, "Here is the Lamb of God who takes away the sin of the world! This is he of whom I said, 'After me comes a man who ranks ahead of me because he was before me.' I myself did not know him; but I came baptizing with water for this reason, that he might be revealed to Israel." And John testified, "I saw the Spirit descending from heaven like a dove, and it remained on him. I myself did not know him, but the one who sent me to baptize with water said to me, 'He on whom you see the Spirit descend and remain is the one who baptizes with the Holy Spirit.' And I myself have seen and have testified that this is the Son of God."

The next day John again was standing with two of his disciples, and as he watched Jesus walk by, he exclaimed, "Look, here is the Lamb of God!" The two disciples heard him say this, and they followed Jesus. When Jesus turned and saw them following, he said to them, "What are you looking for?" They said to him, "Rabbi" (which translated means Teacher), "where are you staying?" He said to them, "Come and see." They came and saw where he was staying, and they remained with him that day. It was about four o'clock in the afternoon. One of the two who heard John speak and followed him was Andrew, Simon Peter's brother. He first found

> his brother Simon and said to him, "We have found the Messiah" *(which is translated Anointed). He brought Simon to Jesus, who looked at him and said, "You are Simon son of John. You are to be called Cephas" (which is translated Peter).*
>
> (John 1:29–42)

It amazes me that whatever the weather, the circumstances, rain, sleet or snow, hell or high water, some people get up on Sunday mornings, ready themselves and come to church. For whatever reason, they just have to come.

Several years ago when I was a pastor in Washington D.C., it snowed in blizzard proportion. I came to church expecting to find no one. Before we were done about 25 people came. We had great worship. The people were few, but we had church. In the 38 years I was pastor at Peoples Church, we never canceled Sunday worship. No matter what the weather or circumstances, the people seemed to come. But why do people come? What are they looking for? What brings them out? No one put a gun to their heads. There is no external compulsion. The question remains: Why do they come? Why are they here?

Church attendance in America has had an interesting history. The Puritans, who were among the early Congregationalists, believed that church attendance should be a matter of law. Therefore, they tried to legislate church attendance by attempting to pass a compulsory church attendance law. If you didn't come to church you would be guilty of a crime, a petty misdemeanor. If one were negligent in church attendance, had the law passed, he or she would have suffered under penalty of law and would have been carried off to prison.

It must also be said that if such a law had passed and prevailed until this day most of our friends and relatives would be in jail. Luckily for us, the Puritans didn't pass a compulsory church attendance law. It smacked too much of the compulsion and restrictions of the Church of England, the rigidity of which the Puritans had come to North American shores to escape. Failing to pass such a law, the Puritans did, however, establish an ethos or an atmosphere, if you prefer, in which missing church was an anti-social act, a breach against civil society. One who missed church was accused of immoral behavior at best, and subject to ridicule and scorn.

Roman Catholic and Protestant Christians in America were a bit different from the Puritans. They did not attempt to legislate church attendance as a part of the civil law. Rather, they made church attendance one of the disciplines of the church. This meant that if you were a good Catholic or a good Methodist or a good Baptist you came to church. That's all there was to it. One who did not attend church was not guilty of a crime against the state but guilty of an infraction against the Christian community. Those who did not attend were regarded to have suffered a character flaw. They were guilty of sin against God and stood in danger of going to hell. Missing church for Catholics and Protestants was pretty heavy stuff.

In our day and in most of our churches, we try to live without these external compulsions. No one forces us, yet we come. So then, the questions remain: Why do we come to church? What are we looking for? Why are we here?

Some would say that we come because it is a social norm. It is of some value to attend church. Coming to church looks like the right thing to do. Church is a good place for a respectable person to be. Others would say that church attendance affords us a cheap social life, and for some it provides ample opportunity for social business and professional contact. Networking, we call it. That's the name of the game for some who come to church.

Some may come to church because it gives them an edge, an upper hand as a respectable person in the larger society. Church attendance seems to be of great value in the marketplace. It is perfectly amazing to me the number of people who place church membership and church office holding on their résumés. Attendance at religious services gives one preference in securing a job, so it would seem. Most people place church attendance in their obituaries too. She attended such-and-such church. These obituaries never say how often the person came or that he or she really came at the behest of his or her spouse.

All in all, people come to church because it is the respectable thing to do. Church attendance is normative social behavior. It gives us an edge on employment, promotions, heaven, and other finer things of life. Church attendance makes people think that we're not half bad, that we are pretty nice guys.

But in any recounting of the history of church attendance in America, it must be said that it is equally as acceptable in our day and time that one need not attend church or synagogue or mosque. If you don't attend church you are still counted among the nice guys. There is not much to compel us

Someone to Follow and a Place to Be

to come to church. What would you think would be the effect of this kind of loose regard for church attendance? If there are no external compulsions that force you to come, what is the result? Would you think it would make church attendance go down? I certainly would. But actually the percentage of the population who attend church in America today is even higher than it was in Colonial times.[1] Isn't that surprising? Church attendance in America today commands a higher percentage of people than at the turn of the 20th century. What do you make of that?

It may surprise you to know that church attendance today is at a rate higher than at the founding of the nation. In terms of the way we like to look at things, in terms of church attendance, the good old days are not in the past. These days in which we live are good days for church attendance in America.

Isn't it the strangest thing you've seen? Without any external compulsions, without rigid discipline, people nevertheless get out of bed on Sunday morning and prepare for church!

But the questions remain: What are you looking for? Whom and what do you seek? Why are you here?

John's telling of the Gospel story of the two disciples who followed after Jesus is important in answering these questions. You will recall that in the Synoptic Gospels—Matthew, Mark, and Luke—Jesus initiates the call to the disciples. As Jesus walks by the Sea of Galilee he sees crude fishermen. He extends the call, and they respond. He bids them follow, and they obey. In the Synoptic Gospels, God in Jesus Christ comes to us out of the blue. The call is God's initiative. The call is

God's search for us. God in Christ is the searching, the seeking God in the Synoptic Gospels.

In the Gospel of John, it is different. In John's Gospel, these were disciples looking for Jesus. The disciples take the initiative. They are curious about Jesus, and so they seek to follow. They literally are walking on Jesus' heels in search of the Master. And Jesus turns around and says to them: "What are you looking for? Why are you following me? Why are you here? Whom do you seek?"

And these would-be disciples who were looking for Jesus said to him, "Teacher, where are you staying?" Now, you can bet your life this was far more than a question about lodging. They didn't want to know if he was staying at the Holiday Inn, Ramada Inn, Days Inn, the "No Room in the Inn," or the "Dew Drop Inn." No, the question "Teacher where are you staying?" is not a question about lodging. Rather, it is a question about the nature of Jesus, the nature of God. They want to know something about the person, the spirit of Jesus.

They followed Jesus on their own initiative. They want to be followers of Jesus and have taken a few steps on their own to be in the right place at the right time to meet this man from Galilee. These disciples follow Jesus because they have a spiritual need to follow him; there is an empty place at the very core of their being; there is a void in their hearts that even John the Baptist had not been able to fill. They come to Jesus tired, weary, and worn-looking for something that bread, money, and natural things will not satisfy. They come because they are all torn apart and are seeking spiritual health and wholeness. They come because they are looking, longing for a rendezvous with God, and they instinctively know that Jesus Christ is the way. Jesus then turns to them asking: "Why are you following me? What are you looking for? Why are you here? Whom do you seek?"

They, in turn, ask Jesus, "Teacher, where do you live?" Now, "where do you live" is an important question. We have always thought we can learn something about a person if we know where they live. "He lives in New York," they say. "That explains a lot." "He's from Atlanta, that's what I thought he would say." We believe you can know a lot about a person if we knew where they were from, where they have been.

We had a saying when I was in college that you could always tell an Alpha man but not very much. If you knew he was an Alpha, Kappa, Omega, Mason, you knew what shape his life was in. If you knew where he lives or where he's coming from and knew something about the source of their spirit, you knew something about who they are.

When I was growing up, before we'd be allowed to visit some other child's home, my mother first had to know who their momma was and where they lived. For my mother this was not a socio-economic question. Instead, it was a question about character, about faith. If I know who your mamma is, where you went to church and where you lived, then I would have a pretty good fix on who you are and where you stand on the ultimate issues of life. If I knew where you lived, I would know something about eternal meanings which form your life, the values which shape you.

"Teacher," they said, "where do you live?" Jesus gave a simple response, "Don't just take my word about where I am coming from or where I live," he said. "Come and see."

Why have you decided to follow Jesus? Why do you come to church? What are you looking for? Whom do you seek? Why are you here? Do you come because it is the law? Of course not. Do you come because it is socially respectable? Perhaps so. Do you come to church because you feel you would go to hell if you didn't? A thousand times no!! We are here because we are looking for someone to follow and a place to be. We are looking for a personhood, a place which grounds our lives and informs us about who we are and to whom we belong.

Uncle Tom, a character out of Harriet Beecher Stowe's historic protest novel, *Uncle Tom's Cabin* is, I believe, one of the most underrated characters in the history.[2] Uncle Tom was actually a fine person of great faith and high character. He was not the pathetic person we have assumed. Once when his master, Simon Legree, caught Tom in an act of disobedience, he decided he would teach Tom a lesson. Simon Legree was determined that Tom would give his ultimate allegiance to him. So he decided to whip him. As he gave Tom many lashes with the whip, upon each stroke the master would ask Tom the question, "Tom, do you know to whom you belong?" And old Tom would answer with a loud cry: "Yes, master. I know to whom I belong." The master was pleased with Tom's answer and his lesson in obedience. But master didn't know all the full meaning of what Tom said. He didn't know what Tom thought with each lash of the whip The master couldn't hear or control Tom's thoughts. Each time Tom said, "Yes master, I know to whom I belong," he thought to himself, "I belong to the Lord Jesus Christ. I belong to the Lord Jesus Christ." Indeed, Tom did know to whom he belonged.

Why do we come to church? Why are you here? Whom do you seek? I believe we come to church because we want to belong to someplace and to be somebody. While our initial motivation may not be the best, I believe we come seeking to belong to the Lord Jesus Christ.

When I was a teenager, I went to church because church had some of the prettiest little girls in town. That was a great incentive to go to church! I also went because my mother made me go and because my father insisted that we go. Attending church was a great habit.

Some people come to church to satisfy their mothers or their wives. Others go to church out of family loyalty: "This was my mother's church and I come here out of loyalty to her." Still others come because church is the cheapest show in town; it's "free entertainment." Our initial motivation for coming to church may not be good, but friends, if we listen up and open our hearts just a little bit, we realize that we need to keep coming, even though we stumble along. We may not at first understand what we're looking for, but if we just hold on, somewhere up the road of coming to church, we discover why we've come—we're here to know whom we seek. We find that we come because we are looking for something to hold on to. We come because we are looking for something and someone to believe in. We come because we are looking for something and somebody big enough and persuasive enough to claim our passions, our devotion, and our faith. We come seeking a shelter against the storms of life. We come looking for a rock in a weary land. We come seeking a challenge to move on up a little bit higher. We come looking for something and someone solid to stand on, someone and something eternal to live for and to live by. We come seeking a community of faith and a community of the faithful. We come looking for Jesus. We come seeking someone to follow and a place to be.

Lord, as Augustine wrote,
you have made us for yourself,
and our hearts are restless
until they find their rest in you.
Amen.

Notes

1. Roger Finke and Rodney Stark, *The Churching of America, 1776–2005: Winners and Losers in Our Religious Economy* (New Brunswick, NJ: Rutgers University Press, 2005).
2. Harriet Beecher Stowe, *Uncle Tom's Cabin: or, Life Among the Lowly* (New York: Penguin Books, 1981).

6

A Stumbling Savior

They compelled a passer-by, who was coming in from the country, to carry his cross; it was Simon of Cyrene, the father of Alexander and Rufus.

(Mark 15:21)

Pop visual artist Andy Warhol once said, "Everyone is entitled to fifteen minutes of fame." This certainly appears to be the case with Simon of Cyrene. Were it not for this one event, we would know nothing about Simon. His fifteen minutes of fame came because he happened to be standing on the street corner as the processional, bearing Jesus to the Cross and to crucifixion on Golgotha's ugly hill, comes by. Simon may be the prototype for a person who is at the scene of the crime when the TV cameras arrive, except he may have been neither a willing witness nor a willing volunteer.

In telling Simon's story, each of the three Synoptic Gospels make it clear that he was "compelled," "seized," "drafted," or "coerced" to help Jesus bear the cross. Other than that, we know so little about Simon. We were told that he was from Cyrene, a province of North Africa, roughly where Libya, the home of the late Saddam Hussein, is today. As a native of North Africa, he may well have been a black man. History never confirms or denies this fact; nonetheless, the likelihood is great that he was a man of color. Besides these few details, little is known about the man who was compelled to bear Christ's cross.

We are not told why he was in Jerusalem. Was he a Jew who had come for the Passover? We don't know. Was he a merchant who had come to sell or buy wares? We don't know. All we know is that he was from Cyrene; that he was the father of Alexander and Rufus, sons equally as unknown as he; and that he was compelled—pressed—into service so that Jesus would not have to bear the cross alone. All we know is that Simon of Cyrene would have forfeited his fifteen minutes of fame had he not been standing in the right place at the right time as Jesus was passing by.

Often, in our press to answer the critical argument about Simon's ethnicity, we overlook the reasons he was compelled—conscripted—to help Jesus bear the cross in the first place.

On a visit to the old city of Jerusalem during my pilgrimage to the Holy Lands, our Israeli guide, Danny, helped us understand why Simon was needed to carry the cross. As he led us on the Via Dolorosa, a narrow walkway, we often came to garish marketplaces where one could buy souvenirs. At a bend in this pathway there were even more vendors selling their wares. Danny pointed to the place where goods were sold and said, "It was there, over by the t-shirts, that Simon of Cyrene was asked to carry the cross of Jesus, because Jesus stumbled."

This was an interesting nuance in the story, but understandable. After the ordeal of the trials and the weight of the cross, Jesus stumbled. Severely weakened because Roman soldiers beat him as he made his way, Jesus stumbled. Somewhere along the way to Golgotha, perhaps over by the t-shirts, the pressure of it all became too much and Jesus stumbled.

The Greek word used to describe the betrayal of Jesus literally means "to be handed over, delivered up, turned in." We find the image of Christ being "handed over" hard to follow. Likewise, the image of Jesus as a stumbling savior may be difficult and hard to follow too. In our culture, where we are desperate to make gods of power and uphold worldly achievement, we don't respect heroes who stumble. In a society which gives us superstars whose feats seem to far exceed our ability to attain, we don't bow down to saviors who stumble.

After retiring from basketball to play baseball, Michael Jordan's return to basketball created frenzy around the country. The stock market actually went up. Our large manufacturers of sporting goods could not keep up with the demands for jerseys with his number. Michael Jordan-ism became the "new religion." I remember witnessing two little boys in a Seven Eleven get all worked up over just seeing a poster of Michael Jordan. They knew everything about him: his records, his points, his salary, everything. I asked one of them, "Why do you like Michael Jordan so much?" "Mister," he replied, "I just love Michael Jordan because he can jump over anything!"

These boys are not alone, for we all seem to love superheroes who appear to be able to jump over anything.

I am one year older than Superman. I grew up with him. All of us little boys hung towels around our necks and went around the neighborhood shouting, "Faster than a speeding bullet! More powerful than a locomotive! Able to leap over tall buildings in a single bound! It's a bird! It's a plane! It's Superman!"

We like heroes who can leap over anything. But we have doubts about saviors who stumble. Had we been on the Via Dolorosa standing near Simon of Cyrene, over by the t-shirts, when Jesus was passing by, we would not have seen a savior who leaped over tall buildings, faster than a speeding bullet, powerful than a locomotive. We would have seen a savior who stumbled, a fallen hero, unsteady by his blood and sweat staining the dust, struggling to stand on his feet, to hold his own. We would have seen soldiers cursing at him, lashing him with whips. We would have seen Jesus staggering under the weight of the cross, bloody and beaten. We may have heard him utter an eighth last word: "Father, I stumble." Oh how difficult it is to rejoice in a savior who stumbles.

Yet, isn't it true that all of us stumble? I've known a lot of stumblers. I've known people fragmented by the persistent demands of family, home, and jobs. They can't seem to wrap themselves around it all. They stumble. "I just can't do all of this anymore," they say. I've known couples sandwiched between caring for their children and their elderly parents, giving all of their time, energy, and resources, receiving little by which to refuel and rebound. I asked them, "What is your

A Stumbling Savior

greatest fear about all of this?" They answered, "Our greatest fear is that we will wake up one morning and have nothing left to give." They fear that they will stumble.

We all stumble under the weight of life's burdens. Some of the greatest, most-accomplished people I've known have stumbled. Henry Emerson Fosdick, the founding pastor of the great Riverside Church in New York City, one of the most outstanding preachers of the 20th century, stumbled. He described his stumble as "bouts of melancholy." Was it clinical depression, bipolar disease, or manic depressive disorder? We don't know. We do know that Henry Emerson Fosdick stumbled. Yet he was able to pick himself up because he knew that it was the human condition to stumble. He knew that it must be alright to stumble like Jesus did.

We have a savior who is like us in every way. He was weak. He bled. He cried out. He stumbled. He died. Jesus is approachable because he is like us in every way, except without sin. If Jesus stumbled, it is alright for us to stumble as we follow Jesus along the way.

One of the reigning people of Washington once said to me, "Church people are like a group of drunks trying to help other drunks get home." I thought to myself that this was one of the biggest compliments ever paid to Christian people. The Church, the society of Jesus, is not a community of folks who can jump over anything. At its best, the church is a gathering of "stumblers," trying to tell others who have fallen how to pick themselves up. The church should be gathered people who bear each other's burdens, who lift the heaviness and pain of another's cross. In the fellowship of Jesus, the one who stumbled, there is room for stumblers like you and me.

Holy Week has always been a rough week for me. If we really observe it, and not try to skip too quickly to the Resurrection, we follow a stumbling Jesus, and we share with him the heaviness of the cross. We follow him as he stumbles along the streets of Jerusalem, as he completely falls over by the t-shirts. We follow his disciples who stumble to the tomb to lay his body away.

So where is the joy in all of this? Perhaps this illustration will help. A wonderful woman and her two sons came by to see me one day in dire need of encouragement and help. The father/husband had left the household with no promise of support. The home was threatened with imminent foreclosure. The future seemed bleak at best. I offered the best advice and encouragement that I could. Then I turned to the two boys and asked, "Do you have any fears about all of this?" The older boy gave a response that could only be characterized as incoherent. As best as I was able to decipher it, his response had to do with the fact that it didn't matter since he had been planning to leave home for some time anyway.

When the younger boy responded, he immediately burst into tears. After we had gone through what seemed like the whole box of Kleenex and he was better composed, I asked him again, "What are your fears?" He responded, "I don't have any fears. We've gone through stuff like this before so I hate to see my mom go through these things again. But Mom is tough. No matter how hard she falls, she picks herself up and always manages to land on her feet."

A Stumbling Savior

Where is the joy in all of this? The joy is in the fact that we worship a stumbling, fallen Savior who was crucified, died, and was buried. He fell as low as he could get but by the grace of God, he managed to pick himself up and land on his feet. For it was early one Sunday morning that the stone was rolled away, he got up, and he landed on his feet. Therein lies the joy of Easter: a stumbling Savior got up, and so can we!

Dear God, as we stumble through life,
we stumble without fear, for we know that you stumbled for us.
We know it is you who extends the helping hand
which picks us up and helps us land on our feet.
Amen.

7

The Real Need of the Given to Give

Now as you excel in everything—in faith, in speech, in knowledge, in utmost eagerness, and in our love for you—so we want you to excel also in this generous undertaking.

I do not say this as a command, but I am testing the genuineness of your love against the earnestness of others. For you know the generous act of our Lord Jesus Christ, that though he was rich, yet for your sakes he became poor, so that by his poverty you might become rich. And in this matter I am giving my advice: it is appropriate for you who began last year not only to do something but even to desire to do something—now finish doing it, so that your eagerness may be matched by completing it according to your means. For if the eagerness is there, the gift is acceptable according to what one has—not according to what one does not have. I do not mean that there should be relief for others and pressure on you, but it is a question of a fair balance between your present abundance and their need, so that their abundance may be for your need, in order that there may be a fair balance. As it is written, "The one who had much did not have too much, and the one who had little did not have too little."

(2 Corinthians 8:7-15)

Three church members were engaged in conversation one day. They talked about how they decided to give in the offering plate each Sunday. The member who was a trustee said that he decided how much to give by drawing a line in the sand. He then would straddle the line and take all the money he made during the week and throw it in the air. The money which fell on the left side of the line was his to keep. What came down to the right of the line belongs to God. He put "God's money" in the offering plate on Sunday.

The second church member was a deacon. To make her decision about how much to give to her church, she drew a circle in the sand about three feet in diameter. At the end of her work week, the deacon took the money she had earned and threw it into the air. What landed in the circle was hers to keep. What landed outside of the circle belonged to God. That's how she decided how much to give.

The third church member served on the church council. Serving on the church council made him just a bit more clever than the deacon and trustee. He thought the method used by them erred on the side of God. He said that each week he took all the money he had earned and didn't hold back a thing. Instead, he threw every last penny into the air. What came down belonged to him, what didn't come down belonged to God. That's what he decided to give to the church.

I am aware of course, that many church members don't like to be reminded of their duty to give of their material resources. Many believe that to speak of money is not spiritual, not biblical. To the contrary, how we use our money is biblical, it is spiritual. How we use our money is a matter of

The Real Need of the Given to Give

religion and faith. If we have made a serious read of the New Testament and if we cut out all the passages that deal with money, the New Testament would look like Swiss cheese. Does it surprise you to know that Jesus talked more about possessions and money than he did about prayer? Money, wealth, and possessions were the subjects that Jesus freely addressed throughout his ministry. In the Old and New Testaments, in page after page, we read discussions about the sharing of wealth and money.

In 2 Corinthians 8:7-15, the passage before us, we find a discussion about money and wealth. In this passage, we find there is a famine in Jerusalem. There were a host of Christians there who were hungry and could not afford the basic necessities of life. In an effort to address the problem of hunger among fellow Christians, Paul wrote letters to the new church he had organized in Turkey and Greece to inform them of the hunger crisis of Christians in Jerusalem. He encouraged them to dig deeply, help out, offer a helping hand, and receive a generous offering for those who had fallen upon hard times.

The church at Philippi responded with a generous gift. It was a small church and very poor. Its communicants were being persecuted because of their faith in Jesus Christ. It was not easy for the small band of poor, persecuted Christians in Philippi to give. Yet in response to the need of fellow Christians in Jerusalem, and in response to the Gospel of Jesus Christ, the Philippian Christians gave.

For the far more wealthy church in Corinth, it was a different story. At the appeal of Paul, the Corinthian Christians didn't send anything immediately. Instead, they took their time, took a vote, and then decided they would make a pledge to give a rather generous gift at a later time. When their donation finally came in it was a very small amount. The Christians at Corinth had pledged to give a generous gift. But when it was finally, begrudgingly sent, the amount was small indeed. Instead of sharing with needy fellow Christians in Jerusalem, they decided to keep most of the money for themselves. Only begrudgingly did they share.

Let's not be too critical of the Christians in Corinth. For truth be told, is there not a tendency among us all to want to keep our money and our material possessions for ourselves?

John Wesley, the founder of the Methodist Movement, taught his followers that they should earn all the money they could. He taught his followers that they should save as much money as they could. But there was a caveat. Wesley taught his followers that they should earn and save not for themselves, but so that they could give as much money as they could to others who had a larger need than themselves.

Some church members strive diligently to earn as much money as they can and some even strive to save as much as they can, but we are reluctant to give what we should in the service of God. Some of us say, of course, that charity begins at home. While that is true, charity shouldn't end there. Charity extends to our brothers and sisters in need, wherever they are found.

Mrs. Eastman of the Eastman Kodak family and fortune was a very wealthy lady. One day her accountant came to her to say she had some bad news. Mrs. Eastman braced her-

The Real Need of the Given to Give

self , after which the accountant informed her that state of New York was going to raise her taxes again that year. Mrs. Eastman responded, "That's not bad news. That's good news. It's good news because if they raise my taxes I can pay for even more children to go to school this year than last year!" Mrs. Eastman had a lot of money but she wasn't obsessed with it. She reached out with her money to help those in need.

By and large our society seems fascinated, even obsessed with money. Popular culture seems energized by money. The prophets of prosperity desecrate the Gospel and use it as a tool to attract money. Money, Money, Money! We want more and more of it, not so that we can help somebody. We want more and more money so that we can help ourselves. We want more and more money to satisfy our insatiable desires.

In his *Letters and Papers from Prison*, Dietrich Bonhoeffer said that Jesus was "the man for others."[1] Dr. Bonhoeffer was right. Jesus lived his life in such a way that even though God had put everything, including all power, in his hands, Jesus didn't keep God's gift for himself. Jesus took everything he had received from God and used it for the sake of others. Jesus was indeed a person for others. Even on the cross, or perhaps especially there, Jesus gave his all.

Our goal as Christians is to be like Jesus and to do like Jesus, so if Jesus gave his all, must we not strive to give our all too?

One of the best measurements of our spirituality is how we're doing when it comes to giving. Our checkbook stubs are more than financial records. Our check stubs are autobiographical statements. Our check stubs tell the story of what we really value in life. If you show me your bank statement, I can learn a lot about who you really are, what you value, and the object of your ultimate concern.

Take a good look at what you give away. If you're only giving one or two percent of your income to the church, it may very well mean that you are playing around with God and are not serious about the Christian faith. If you give just a little bit, examine your life, not just your giving, because your giving might be a sign that God isn't the center of your life. The Old Testament suggests that we should give ten percent of our income to God as a return of thanks, as a return on God's investment in us.

Most of us talk a good God game. We sing and talk of our great love of God and our love of Jesus Christ. And yet, when it comes to giving we show little or no care and love of God at all.

Years ago there was a show in the radio called *The Beulah Show*. The main character, Beulah, had a boyfriend named Bill. One night in a telephone call, Bill pledged his undying love for Beulah. He said, "Beulah, don't you know, I'd climb the highest mountain or swim the deepest ocean for you?" Just as he was about to hang up, he said, "By the way, Beulah, I'll be by to see you this evening if it don't rain."

We so often pledge our deepest love to God. We promise to give God our best and our all. But when it comes to sharing, we tell God that the money which stays in the air belongs to God. Even as we pledge our all to God, we tell God that we'll do all God wants us to do, as long as the creek doesn't rise and it doesn't rain.

The offering we give to our various churches is not simply to enable us to pay the electric bill, the gas bill, the janitors, and the preachers. In a real sense, the offering we give each Sunday is a spiritual opportunity, a barometer, a measuring rod which shows where God stands in our lives.

The Rev. Edward Harrington, who for many years was pastor of the Peachtree Street Presbyterian Church in Atlanta, used to tell the story of an old man who was extremely hard of hearing and came to church every Sunday. One day Pastor Harrington said to the old man, "Charlie, you are so hard of hearing. Why do you come to church at all?" The old man was so hearing impaired that the pastor had to write his words to the man so that he could understand. "Why, do you come to church, Charlie? You can't hear the prayers, you can't hear the sermon, can't hear the Scriptures, the anthems, or the hymns. Why do you come at all?" Charlie replied to Pastor Harrington, "Pastor, you're right, I can't hear the prayers, hymns, sermons, or the Word of God, but I come to church each and every Sunday anyway just to show God whose side I'm on."

The offering on Sunday morning is an opportunity for the faithful to show where God stands in our lives and where we stand in the life of God. Our giving is a valid sign that shows God and the world whose side we're on.

Jesus said, "Where your treasure is, there your will be heart also" (Matthew 6:21). Remember to open up your hearts, and give even as Christ has given to you.

> *O Giver of Life and every perfect gift,*
> *open our hearts to give generously to those in need.*
> *We can never repay the gift you have given to us.*
> *Our meager offering is but a small return*
> *on all that you have invested in us.*
> *Receive it now, we pray.*
> *Amen.*

Note

1. Dietrich Bonhoeffer, *Letters and Papers from Prison* (New York: Touchstone, 1953), 382.

8

One in the Spirit—One in the Lord

John said to him, "Teacher, we saw someone casting out demons in your name, and we tried to stop him, because he was not following us." But Jesus said, "Do not stop him; for no one who does a deed of power in my name will be able soon afterward to speak evil of me. Whoever is not against us is for us. For truly I tell you, whoever gives you a cup of water to drink because you bear the name of Christ will by no means lose the reward.

"If any of you put a stumbling block before one of these little ones who believe in me, it would be better for you if a great millstone were hung around your neck and you were thrown into the sea. If your hand causes you to stumble, cut it off; it is better for you to enter life maimed than to have two hands and to go to hell, to the unquenchable fire. And if your foot causes you to stumble, cut it off; it is better for you to enter life lame than to have two feet and to be thrown into hell. And if your eye causes you to stumble, tear it out; it is better for you to enter the kingdom of God with one eye than to have two eyes and to be thrown into hell, where their worm never dies, and the fire is never quenched.

"For everyone will be salted with fire. Salt is good; but if salt has lost its saltiness, how can you season it? Have salt in yourselves, and be at peace with one another."

(Mark 9:38-50)

Several years ago, I was asked to perform a wedding ceremony on an old plantation just outside Manassas, Virginia. It was a glorious event. The couple, aware that I had recently had a hip joint replacement, sent a car and driver to pick me up. The wedding took place shortly after the tragic events of 9/11. The driver looked as if he could have been one of the sons of Saddam Hussein. I found this somewhat disconcerting, if not frightening. So all the way to Manassas from Washington, D.C and back, I had to confront my own personal prejudices and to remind myself how foolish, how brainwashed I have become. Everybody who has a Middle Eastern look, I reminded myself, is not out to do me harm.

Somehow, most of us have developed strange sensibilities. We believe that anyone who doesn't look like us, speak as we speak, and believe as we believe, may in fact be the enemy and may neither be trusted nor endured. A major cause of our easy invasion of Iraq is a thinly veiled ethnocentrism, if not racism, which says that since these people are not like us, we can bomb them to pieces and hardly look back.

We, of the church, are not immune from the tendency to dismiss those who are not like us. In the Gospel lesson, John, one of the disciples of Jesus said to him, "Master, we saw a man casting out devils in your name; he is not one of us. He doesn't look like us. He doesn't speak like us—therefore we tried to stop him from casting out demons." Jesus said to John and the other disciples, "Do not try to stop him. Let him do his good works, for anyone who is not against us is for us." Jesus said to John, "Be tolerant of those who don't look like us, who don't speak like us, for anyone who does good, anyone who does what God wills, is on our side."

Somehow, those of us who are a part of the Church of Jesus Christ have forgotten Jesus' little sermon on inclusion and tolerance. We don't seem as driven as we once were to repair the breach between people of different religious traditions and faiths. Christians, Muslims, Jews, Buddhists, and Hindus seem more than divided than ever. And who can deny that Christianity is splintered into a million pieces? We are divided into a thousand different denominations.

In today's lesson, Jesus admonishes us to be tolerant of each other. In fact, we are to find complicity and cooperation with all who do Christ's work whether they do it in the name of Jesus or not.

This is an important lesson for Christians to learn. Today we live in a global community. People from Vietnam, Ghana, Mexico, Columbia, France, and hundreds of other nations are not in some distant land; they are a part of the very neighborhoods in which we live. Through the miracle of the internet and the telephone we have immediate access to people all over the world. We should seek to join with any of them who promote what is good, beautiful, just, and true, whether they are of our ethnicity or religious persuasion or not. Jesus said those who are not against us are on our side.

In my ministry in the nation's capital, the church I served was a member of the downtown cluster of congregations. The cluster was a diverse assembly of Christians, Jews, and Muslims who came together to try to do what was best for the future of our city. The cluster was also inclusive of Baptists,

Catholics, United Church of Christ Churches, Presbyterians, Methodist, Episcopalians, Pentecostals Assemblies of God, Seventh-day Adventists, and a host of other Christian denominations. Theologically we may not have been of one accord, but we were of one spirit and one mind when it came to doing what is good and right and just for the District of Columbia.

In this day and time, Christians must not be afraid to be tolerant of those on the outside of our fellowship who are engaged in good things like healing and serving the hungry and the homeless. We must be open to all people who do well.

Many years ago, my son Nathaniel was in the hospital at the point of death. We provided for him the best medical therapy we could afford. I had prayed and prayed that God would restore him to health. I solicited the prayers of others. But nothing seemed to pull him out of what seemed to be a catatonic and often comatose state. One day when I got to his room, there stood over him a small woman with Asian features. She was a nun—one who still wears the habit of a nun, including that strange little cover for the head. At first I was offended that this lady of another Christian denomination, another faith tradition, would stand over my child and presume to pray for him without a proper introduction, without permission. I was offended because I felt that she felt that my Protestant prayer may not be as effective as hers. But as I observed the dynamic between the two of them, I came to feel that she was essential to his health. They had connected. As ill as he was, Nathaniel seemed to strain toward her. He seemed drawn to her face as if he saw a divine light. Each day I visited with him, there was this nun, Korean by nationality, a sister of the Missionaries of Charity, the order of Mother Teresa. A disciple of Jesus Christ was standing over him praying, reciting the rosary. She seemed to do him good. More and more each day, Nathaniel strained toward her as he slowly came back to life. One day he reached out and touched her face. She said to him, "Nathaniel, we are not supposed to let you touch us, but I let you touch me because in my face you seem to see the face and the light of God."

Indeed, he did. The next day he was even better! He not only reached out and touched her face, but he pulled up in his bed for the first time in at least a month and gave this tiny little nun a hug as both of them wept. And as if that were not enough, the very next day my son was taken from the critical list. When I visited with him he was sitting up in a chair in his hospital room, able to eat, to speak, and to laugh for the first time in weeks. I felt that this strange little Missionary of Charity was Nathaniel's guardian angel who brought him out of darkness into light, who brought him out of the wilderness and who saw him through.

In our day and time Christians must know that the Gospel of Jesus Christ and the good works of the Lord Jesus Christ transcend all religious boundaries and people of faith. Even those of faiths different from our own experience the power and presence of God, although they do not call it by the name of Jesus Christ. In the 21st century, Christians need to understand that anyone who is not against the ministry we try to do is not our enemy. We are on the same side, the same team.

We must not only be tolerant of those outside our faith— we must also be tolerant of those who share our faith. Some of us think that the best form of Christianity is that which we practice. We so often think that the best belief system is that belief system and the theology we believe. I have had other clergy question my call into ministry because my call didn't come in the same way their call came. We simply do not all experience the call of Christ in the same way. In both the church and the world, we are not all called to the same work of Christ. In the fourth chapter of the book of Ephesians we are reminded that God gives us different gifts: "The gifts he gave were that some would be apostles, some prophets, some evangelists, some pastors and teachers, to equip the saints for the work of ministry, for building up the body of Christ, until all of us come to the unity of the faith and of the knowledge of the Son of God, to maturity, to the measure of the full stature of Christ" (Ephesians 4:11-13). We need to know that God never intended that we should all be gifted in the same way. God never intended that all of us would serve in the same way. God never intended that we would all believe and be the same thing. God intended that it is all of us together believing and being and doing in the way that the Holy Spirit inspires each of us who make up the church, the whole body of Christ.

One of the things which divide Christian churches is the music. Somewhere along the line we've come to believe that only my kind of music can be raised in authentic praise of God. I believe that God enjoys and accepts all kinds of music which is sung in praise of God. We don't have to sing the same songs or be on the same beat to celebrate the life we share in Jesus Christ. But if our hearts and minds are truly stayed on

Jesus, we sing from the same page and our rejoicing is of one accord.

Some are good at Bible study and theological and intellectual discussions. Others are better at frying chicken and baking pies. If we have the mind of Christ within us, whatever gifts we offer, large or small, are acceptable and received with gratitude by the Lord our God. Christians must recognize that God not only gave us different gifts, but God gave us gifts in different measure, all to be used to the glory of God.

In my years as a pastor, I saw members of trustee boards who were faithful and abundantly loyal and able for the task of trustees. But they would have been a disaster, at a complete loss, if we sent them off to teach Sunday school.

I remember one Sunday morning as a deacon prayed in worship, and my mind wandered a bit. I'll never know how or why my mind became unfocused. Rather than becoming attuned with the deacon in prayer, I began to wonder if the brother could cook. I wondered if he could fry chicken, grill a steak, or bake bread. When I found myself wondering and so far gone, I said to myself, it really doesn't matter if the deacon can or cannot cook, but this I know: the deacon sure can pray. He can lift up his voice and bring heaven down. He may not be good in the kitchen, but he is a prince before the throne of grace.

A strong Christian community is inclusive of everyone who does God's will and knows how to place a person where they can give of their best to the master and shine to the glory of God.

John Milton ends his poem titled "On His Blindness," saying, "they also serve who only stand and wait." So many times, we as Christian communities believe that only those who looked worthy served God. We want to get everyone busy. We want everybody to be a trustee or a deacon, to sing in the choir, teach Sunday school, go to Bible study, mow the lawn, chair a committee, or do something! Like Martha, we want the Marys of this world who do absolutely nothing but sit at the feet of Jesus to get busy. We want those who do nothing but sit in church and leave when service is over to get off their duffs and do something to advance the ministry of Jesus Christ and the kingdom of God. But isn't there a point at which we have to agree with John Milton that they also serve who only sit. Church leaders need to be patient and understanding of those who only stand or sit and wait.

When I was a young pastor in Detroit, there was a man who came to the early service at our church late and left early, so that he would not have to meet or speak to anyone. Nobody in our congregation seemed to know him. Like the Lone Ranger, he never took time to identify himself, leaving us wondering who he was. After about six months of coming late and leaving early, one Sunday this unidentified man finally stayed after the service. A gracious man of about 40 years, he introduced himself. He said how glad he was that he found our church. He said, "I was going through the deepest crisis of my life. You cannot know how much healing came from the Word of God as I sat there in the deepest pain of the soul trying to find healing for myself."

At that point in his life, he didn't want to do anything in the church. He didn't even want to speak to anyone. He just wanted to sit there in search of a healing word from the Lord.

Indeed, it is time to recognize that some who only stand and wait still serve. Congregations know this and provide room, provide an environment in which people, led by the spirit, minister, not to others, but to themselves.

The greatest challenge before us in the present age is to be inclusive and to minister to the whole people of God. The Gospel of Jesus Christ transcends all boundaries, and those who are not against Jesus are on his side. But we also must be tolerant of each other, which is a part of the society of Jesus. It takes us one and all to be the body of Christ. And we must always understand that God loves and accepts each of us—even those who only stand and wait.

Dear God, draw me closer to you
so that I may be drawn even closer
to those who may not know the name of Jesus.
All of us have come to you, O God,
men and women, all races, tongues, creeds, and nations
in your mighty works of good will.
Amen.

9

No More Walls

So then, remember that at one time you Gentiles by birth, called "the uncircumcision" by those who are called "the circumcision"—a physical circumcision made in the flesh by human hands—remember that you were at that time without Christ, being aliens from the commonwealth of Israel, and strangers to the covenants of promise, having no hope and without God in the world. But now in Christ Jesus you who once were far off have been brought near by the blood of Christ. For he is our peace; in his flesh he has made both groups into one and has broken down the dividing wall, that is, the hostility between us. He has abolished the law with its commandments and ordinances, that he might create in himself one new humanity in place of the two, thus making peace, and might reconcile both groups to God in one body through the cross, thus putting to death that hostility through it. So he came and proclaimed peace to you who were far off and peace to those who were near; for through him both of us have access in one Spirit to the Father. So then you are no longer strangers and aliens, but you are citizens with the saints and also members of the household of God, built upon the foundation of the apostles and prophets, with Christ Jesus himself as the cornerstone. In him the whole structure is joined together and grows into a holy temple in

> the Lord; in whom you also are built together spiritually into a dwelling place for God.
>
> (Ephesians 2:11-22)

Robert Frost's poems are a part of fabric of American culture. This is especially true of his poem "Mending Wall."[1] Now our American classic, this poem concerns a stone wall between the poet's property and that of a neighbor. Mr. Frost and his neighbor seemed to be constantly mending the wall by replacing the stones that have fallen from it. The stones stubbornly refused to stay in place. The poet and his neighbor are at odds as to the place—if any—that fences and walls should hold in society. The neighbor believed that they are good and necessary. They keep people separated and divided so as to minimize contact and conflict. "Good fences," he concluded, "make good neighbors." Mr. Frost took issue with his neighbor. He believed that there is something at the very core of nature and the scheme of reality that is at odds with walls and fences. The universe resists walls that separate and divide. He believed that there is a power in the universe which detests fences, which wants them down.

Now, while I have one of the tallest, most imposing stone fences in my neighborhood, there is something about what Robert Frost said that rings true. Good fences do not make good neighbors. There is something in the universe, something in the very nature of reality, which fences do to the Ephesians and to Robert Frost, who are of the same frame of mind. The Epistle writer, however, personifies the "power" which allows walls. He says there is not something but someone in nature of what is real who doesn't like fences and walls. There is someone at the core of all that is who wants walls down. Clearly, for the writer of Ephesians, that someone who knocks down walls that separate us is Jesus Christ. It is Jesus who has torn down the walls that separate humankind.

With his own body and blood, Christ has broken down and taken away the fences and walls which divide us and separate humankind. Christ has created a new humanity—where class, ethnic background, race, nationality, gender, sexual orientation, and religion no longer have the power to divide. All of us, therefore, are full citizens of the city of God with all of the rights, privileges, responsibilities, and obligations appertaining thereto.

Several years ago, I was in attendance at the General Synod of the United Church of Christ which was convened in Minneapolis, Minnesota. The General Synod, the national gathering of my denomination, meets every two years. The delegates to the Synod are elected by the conference and then gather to make decisions that are of consequence both to the church and the world. The General Synod is noted worldwide for taking liberal positions on social issues. After biblical and theological reflection on the issues, the delegates to the Synod take a stand. The position they take speaks to the people rather than for them.

I've always been pleased with the positions that this particular General Synod has taken. I was not a delegate to the Synod when it convened so I did not get to vote on the issues. But as a part of its process, registered guests at the Synod can participate in small-group, non-plenary discussion of the issues. These discussions help clarify the issues and are a resource to delegates as they prepare to vote. Ten young people from Peoples Congregational United Church of Christ were among these who were on panel in Minneapolis. I was pleased to see how engaged these young people were on the discussion. They were very faithful to the task and were forthcoming in making their views known. In the United Church of Christ, we are a diverse people. What an experience it was for these youth!

It was also wonderful experience for me to greet once again acquaintances, colleagues, and friends I've come to know and love over many years. They are such a microcosm of the American tapestry. Take, for example, my friend Irving. He was one of the first people with whom I became reunited at the Synod. Retired now, he had been the editor of my hometown newspaper, *The Greensboro Daily News*. Irving was well into his seventies by then, a white man with a Southern accent as thick and dark as molasses. He had been a reporter when I first knew him in Greensboro some 40 years before. He covered the historic Greensboro Sit-in Movement in the early 1960s.

Irving said, "Greensboro is wonderful in every way. Because students were willing to risk giving their bodies and blood to break down the walls and fences which divided black from white, Greensboro is a far better place." And I said to him, "Right Irving, isn't that what Christ has done for us on the cross? Didn't Christ break down the walls that divided, the fences which separated us?" Irving responded. "Yes, he did. You know he did." Irving and I embraced each other, cried tears of joy for a moment, and went on our way. We were one in the spirit one in the Lord. Between us there were no walls

Indeed, there is someone in the universe who doesn't have walls and who wants them down. That someone is Jesus Christ. I could celebrate the General Synod because over the years, it has been obedient to a Christ who wants no walls.

The next person I ran across was Reverend Joseph Evans. Joe was 87 years old at the time. He lives in Florida in the winter and on Martha's Vineyard in the summer. Joe had the distinction of being the only African American who had held the highest office in the United Church of Christ. Joe was in one of those funny little scooters that those of us with various impairments of the hips and knees and ankles have to use from time to time. When I saw Joe Evans, my right hip was totally out of joint and I too was riding in one of those little scooters. Joe Evans was a name I've known all my life since Joe is 21 years older than I. The age made a difference. At national meetings, because of the age and experience difference, Joe had little to say to me. He was always busy with many things. When I was younger, I wondered if he ever knew my name. While I stood in such awe of him, I regretted that we had not really connected in years past. When I saw Joe, I expected to be greeted of course, but only briefly, and then courteously dismissed. I expected to move forward in my little scooter and press on. But Joe clung to me. He shed a tear or two and told me how glad he was to see me, and how he and I were the only two African American "old timers" left. I agreed that he was right. I was honored to be an "old timer" with Joe, and at last to be his colleague, his peer, and his friend in Jesus Christ.

Joe and I sat in our little carts holding hands, reminiscing and admiring each other, as what seemed like a thousand photographers snapped pictures of us. We too were one in the spirit, one in the Lord. Thank God that there is someone in the universe who does not like fences that have been built because of generation and age. That someone is Jesus Christ.

One afternoon at General Synod I was to appear on a panel at a distant hotel. The adult members of my party had concluded that because of my age and physical condition, I was unable to go anywhere unaccompanied, so they chose Aaron Mack, one of the youth from Peoples Church, to be my escort. Aaron was perhaps the youngest of our youth. He had a knack for asking peculiar questions and saying strange things. Because he had taken seriously his instruction to see me safely to my destination, we likely offended a lot of people by the time we got to the meeting room.

I did well on the panel. As the moderator was about to conclude the meeting, a woman with a southern accent stood and said, "May I speak as a matter of personal privilege?" The moderator graciously gave her permission to speak. She said, "I must say something to Tony Stanley." I said to myself, "Oh, I hope I didn't offend her." She pressed on. "Tony may not remember me, but we met nearly 50 years ago at Grinnell College in Grinnell, Iowa. You were the president of the African American youth of our denomination in the South, and I was the president of the white youth of our denomination in the South. Although we lived only 35 miles from each other in North Carolina, we had never met before. We met in Grinnell, Iowa, at a meeting of youth. At that meeting, Tony and I pledged that if it took a lifetime, we would tear down the walls that divided us racially, especially in the church, and in our own way we have done precisely that." Then she said, "I'm Faye Gordon from Charlotte, North Carolina, and other than the woman who cleaned my mother's house, Tony was the first African American I had ever met. Do you remember me?"

I responded, "Yes, Faye, I do remember you. I remember another boy, Millard Fuller, who was also at that meeting. Millard Fuller was also changed at Grinnell and went on to found Habitat for Humanity. Faye, I, too, thank God for the Church of Jesus Christ which brought us together across the boundaries of race and clan." What a great reunion that was! Faye and I wept tears of joy and all in that room rejoiced with us.

I came away from General Synod as I always come, thanking God that I belong to a denomination which follows the mind of Christ. I came away thanking God that I belong to a denomination that strives to include everyone regardless of race, class, nationality, gender, sexual orientation, or manners of belief. But most especially, I came away from General Synod thanking God that I belong to someone who doesn't like fences. I belong to someone who despises walls and wants them to come down. I belong to someone who is our peace. That someone is **JESUS CHRIST**, the son of the God of love who in that love tears down fences and walls. I invite you to give yourself to Christ and to belong to this someone, too.

*God, I thank you for opportunities
to tear down the fences which divide your people.
I thank you that you are God who tears down the fences
of collective sin which separate us
from you and from each other.
I thank you that we belong to you.
Amen.*

Note

1. Robert Frost, "Mending Wall," *Tendencies in Modern American Poetry* (New York: Macmillan Co., 1920).

10

The Importance of Memory in Difficult Times

But we must always give thanks to God for you, brothers and sisters beloved by the Lord, because God chose you as the first fruits for salvation through sanctification by the Spirit and through belief in the truth. For this purpose he called you through our proclamation of the good news, so that you may obtain the glory of our Lord Jesus Christ. So then, brothers and sisters, stand firm and hold fast to the traditions that you were taught by us, either by word of mouth or by our letter.

Now may our Lord Jesus Christ himself and God our Father, who loved us and through grace gave us eternal comfort and good hope, comfort your hearts and strengthen them in every good work and word.

(2 Thessalonians 2:13-17)

In this meditation, I want to reflect on the importance of memory. I find that as one grows older one realizes that while short-term memory may diminish, the kind of memories that stick to the heart and gut seem to visit at frequent intervals. I'm speaking of the kind of memories that shape life—memories which "from our mothers' arms [have] blessed us on our way, with countless gifts of love, and still is ours today."[1] One of the memories that have shaped me is the memory of international conflict, the memory of wars. Planted deeply in my childhood memory are memories of World War II.

Wars are far too complicated for children or even adults to understand. My childhood world was very small. It extended only nine miles away from my parents' home to the next town. That was the extent of both my travels and my world. Yet I was convinced that World War II was being fought within those nine miles. You can imagine how frightened and threatened I felt. The enemy for me could be lurking behind every bush. Darkness was the enemy's friend. In her, he could hide.

By early teens, my world had expanded. The Korean War became a part of the landscape of my memory. But even with an enlarged geographic vision of my world, I didn't understand why we were fighting a war halfway across the big world. I particularly did not understand why my older brother, Joseph, had been compelled, drafted to fight in that war. North Koreans were not enemies to him. I only knew that it was said that the Korean War was being fought to contain Communism to make the world safe for democracy.

The Vietnam War also jolts my memory. What a stretch for me and other young people to justify that nasty, bloody war. The toll it took upon the soul of our nation and upon the quality of life of those who engaged in it is too vast to be measured. Our sense of moral meaning as a people lay in the bal-

The Importance of Memory in Difficult Times

ance as regards this war. There it stubbornly remained waiting to be tipped. Wars and rumors of wars continue: The Gulf Wars; the Iraq War; the War in Afghanistan; the War against Terrorism. Sadly, I tell you, the history of my own memories can be told in terms of war.

It is not the duty, however, of those of us who are charged with proclaiming the Gospel to remember the history of an enterprise that may or may not be. Rather it is our duty to proclaim to you that at the heart of Christian faith, practice, and belief is the call to remembrance. It is our duty to say to you that in a real sense to be a Christian, a follower of Jesus Christ, is an experience in memory.

My earliest of all memories—even before the memory of war—is that of waking up in a country church on a Sunday morning enfolded in the loving and affectionate arms of my older sister, Joye. I remember there was the fresh smell of azalea in the air. There were hymns joyously sung and prayers earnestly prayed. But most of all there was the love of my sister. I knew, even from a childlike perspective, that whatever else that experience meant, its most profound meaning was GOD. For me, being a Christian is an exercise in memory. It is waking up in church on Sunday morning; it is the memory of God.

But this exercise in memory, in the context of our religion, takes us far beyond our own personal memory of our individual faith journey and experience. The kinds of memory which really make us Christians are those memories which encompass the written and oral traditions of our Judeo-Christian traditions, as well as those of our mothers and fathers in the faith.

In the Epistle lesson before us, Paul tells the Christians in the church at Thessalonica to hold fast to the tradition which you have been taught. Paul tells them to hold fast to the memory, the profound faith tradition out of which you have come. Hold fast to your memory of the wonderful stories of your fathers and mothers in the faith.

It is important for us to know that Paul called on the Christians of Thessalonica to hold fast to their remembrance of the faith in a time that was not unlike the time in which we presently live. Uncertainty loomed all around them. Yet Paul tells them to be glad in the midst of this outbreak of uncertainty. Roman persecution of Christians was becoming rampant. Christians were constantly under attack. They lived in constant fear for their lives, wondering if the day of the Lord would soon come. They wondered if the day of the Lord, long-awaited by people of faith, would come, and there would be an outbreak of peace; a day when there would be domestic tranquility; when there would be good food to eat and lambs lying down with lions; a time when there would be dancing in the streets.

It was under these circumstances that Paul said to the Christians at Thessalonica that the day of the Lord will indeed come at some future time. The day and time are not for us to know. But until the day of the Lord comes, we have to keep the faith. We have to keep hope alive. Therefore, you must hold fast to the tradition which you have been taught. Paul understood, in a way that we often forget, that at the heart of

The Importance of Memory in Difficult Times

Christian belief is a call to remembrance. Paul understood in a way that we often forget that to be a Christian is an exercise in memory.

Memory is of essential importance to the ongoing journey of human life. I knew a man who claimed that he remembered the day of his birth. When we challenged him, he would tell us what he remembered about that day. He was positive that he remembered the day of his birth because, as a minister's son, he was born in a house right next door to the church. In all sincerity, this otherwise intelligent man claimed that he remembered that the church burned down on the very day of his birth.

The experts tell us that memory so early in life is impossible. Both physical and intellectual developments are too elementary to entertain memory when we are so young. This man could not have remembered the day of his birth. He had no experience to hang it on.

But I want to tell you that although it is physically and intellectually impossible to remember what happened on the day of our births, if we cannot remember a past which precedes our births, we are not only orphans, we are lost. If we cannot remember and claim a past which precedes our birth we become uprooted in a world in which the very foundations of the earth do tremble.

Two women who were members of Peoples Congregational United Church of Christ in D.C. once were teasing me about the stories I told in sermons. In their teasing, each challenged the accuracy of my memory. Another wondered if my stories were true. "How do you remember back so far?" she asked. I told her my stories are substantially true. I admitted however, that I tweak the stories a bit. I add a little here and take away a little there. Sometimes I change gender, time, and place so that no one can possibly guess of whom I'm speaking or who I'm remembering. But my stories are essentially true.

The other woman said she used to say about some of my stories, "We've heard that story before." I'd forgotten that I told it. One Sunday I said in my sermon while repeating an often-told story: "I know you all have heard this story before, but after all how many stories does one person have or even remember?" After that confession, she has forgiven me whenever I've told one of my stories over and over again.

The truth of the matter is that these stories are not just an exercise in memory. Rather when I recall them and the people in them, I become the creation of all that these stories and the people in them mean to me. I do not blithely tell these stories. I need to tell these stories; I must tell these stories if I am to keep track of who I am. If I am to remember what I value, if I am always to be mindful of to Whom I belong in life, I must tell these stories. These stories are the memories which connect me to that which gives me real life again.

I must have told the story of my great-uncle Hugh in ten different sermons. I tell it from the pulpit because I have to remind myself that I belong to this ancient man, an old Alabama "colored" man, poor as Job's turkey but who was nonetheless rich. He was rich because he would give you his last dime. He'd give you his last dime because he trusted that God had more resources for him in the storehouse of God's love. He believed he would never go wanting. I am compelled to

The Importance of Memory in Difficult Times

remember my uncle Hugh because he is one of the fathers of my faith. Were it not for my memory of him, I would become uprooted during an outbreak of uncertainty. I would become unglued in troubled times.

As long as I live, I must tell the story of Uncle Hugh because I am who I am because I remember who he was. You see, in this world, we are what we remember.

A Native American of the Kiowa tribe tells the story that as a young boy he was taken to the cottage of an old Kiowa woman, where for the better part of ten days she told him the history of his tribe in story and in song. He said that when he left the old woman after those days he was no longer just a playful, drifting, aimlessly little boy; he was indeed a Kiowa Indian. He had become what this old woman had remembered of the history of his people and tribe.

Indeed, we become what we remember. If we forget the old stories which have shaped our past and the past of our people, we become victims of the future. We become defeated in uncertain times. We can gain strength through what we remember or we can become "unbridged" over trouble waters.

I remember how painful it was for me to conduct the memorial service of my older brother, Bill. To experience his transition from labor to reward was almost more than I could bear. But the upside of it all is that the occasion of his death gave me a wonderful opportunity to begin to remember all that he was and meant to me. Good funerals are those in which we remember. Measured in that way, my brother's funeral was exceptional. His death not only brought memories of him, but also memories of those moments of the past which have shaped me. The stories of my childhood, early and late, flooded my memory that day. These stories and memories have shaped my life.

One of the memories which frequently comes upon me is my last visit to my family home. Mother and father had both gone on. The old home place had been sold and would soon have a new tenant. My wife, Andrea, and I were driving through Greensboro and my sister invited us to go into the house and choose from among the few things left, a keepsake or two that we would like to have as mementos to help us remember them. When we entered the house, it was all but empty. All the larger furniture—gone; the good smell of food cooking—gone; my parents' voices—gone. Yet the house was still full of memories. I remembered my parents at the table as the family gathered. I remembered sitting around the fireplace late at night with good homemade snacks to eat while we played all kinds of quiet games. I remember five children singing around the piano. I remember where my mother displayed her bric-a-brac—things of her precious memories. Of all the assorted items left, I wanted only two things: the marker which contained the numbers of the family home address and a large glass sugar bowl which my parents had received as a wedding gift some sixty years before.

As we were about to leave, I was holding fast to the old home address and the sugar bowl, and looking back at the empty house in great forlorn and pain I said to Andrea, "There isn't much left, is there?" Andrea said to me with a certain authority and wisdom that she can sometimes give: "You have everything left. You have a fine upbringing and the memory of godly parents who were fine exemplars of faithfulness and faith."

Whenever I grow faint in life, I remember this Godly heritage, and when I remember, I can stand up to life. For, you see, we are what we remember.

Years ago, Langston Hughes wrote a poem titled "The Negro Speaks of Rivers," in which he portrays the idea that the history of African people in America can be told in terms of our collective memory of our experience of rivers. I recited this poem before assembly in junior high school years ago. It was my first public presentation. I used it in the eulogy for my brother because it ties us all to a memory we share.

> I've known rivers:
>
> I've known rivers ancient as the world and older than the flow of human blood in human veins.
>
> My soul has grown deep like the rivers.
>
> I've bathed in the Euphrates when dawns were young.
>
> I built my hut near the Congo and it lulled me to sleep.
>
> I looked upon the Nile and raised the pyramids above it.
>
> I heard the singing of the Mississippi when Abe Lincoln went down to New Orleans, and I've seen its muddy bosom turn all golden in the sunset.
>
> I've known rivers:
>
> Ancient, dusty rivers.
>
> My soul has grown deep like rivers.[2]

We are what we remember. If you don't remember where you come from, you have no idea where you're going. If you become disconnected from the memory of your heritage, you become unglued. Faith is memory and if you have no memory you have so little faith.

It is of the utmost importance, therefore, that we remember the tradition which is our faith. Paul reminds us to hold fast to the traditions of faith that we have been taught. Paul admonishes us to hold fast to our tradition, our memory of the faith, because at the very heart of Christian belief is a call to remember. Paul reminds us that to be a Christian is an exercise in memory. If we forget the old stories of the faith, we become victims of the future; we become defeated in uncertain times.

As Christian people who claim the traditions, the memory of our faith, we must never forget how God brought us out of bondage in Egypt, how we crossed the sea on dry land. As people who claim the traditions, we must never forget how God brought us out of exile in Babylon and reestablished us as a nation. As faithful Christians, we must always remember, that, indeed, we were there when they crucified my Lord, we were there when they laid him in his tomb,[3] and above all else, we must always remember that we were there when he rose from the dead. Through the memory of that death and resurrection we are re-created, renewed, and brought again to the fullness of life. We must always remember.

> *We ask you, O God, to remember us*
> *through the good and bad times alike.*

We also ask that you remind us to remember you.
Remind us that in all the ventures of our lives
and in the life of your faithful people of all ages,
tongues, and races, even in our old age
when we don't remember much,
sustain us with memories of you
and memories of the sacrifice of Christ.
Amen.

Notes

1. Martin Rinckart, "Now Thank We All Our God."

2. Langston Hughes, "The Negro Speaks of Rivers," *The Collected Poems of Langston Hughes*, Arnold Rampersad and David Roessel, eds. (New York: Alfred A. Knopf, 1959), 23. This poem was first published in 1921 in *Crisis* magazine.

3. "Were You There (When They Crucified My Lord)," spiritual in public domain.

11

Having Church

This was Rev. Stanley's last public sermon which was preached at First Congregational UCC in Atlanta, Georgia, on Sunday, September 9, 2012.

As the Father has loved me, so I have loved you; abide in my love. If you keep my commandments, you will abide in my love, just as I have kept my Father's commandments and abide in his love. I have said these things to you so that my joy may be in you, and that your joy may be complete.

"This is my commandment, that you love one another as I have loved you. No one has greater love than this, to lay down one's life for one's friends. You are my friends if you do what I command you. I do not call you servants any longer, because the servant does not know what the master is doing; but I have called you friends, because I have made known to you everything that I have heard from my Father. You did not choose me but I chose you. And I appointed you to go and bear fruit, fruit that will last, so that the Father will give you whatever you ask him in my name. I am giving you these commands so that you may love one another.

(John 15:9-17)

In the ninth verse of the 15th chapter of the Gospel of John, Jesus said, "As the Father has loved me, so I have loved you; abide (continue) in my love."

There is a sense in which this one verse serves as a summary of the entire Gospel as John understood it. In the Gospel of John, truly it is love that shapes the life of Jesus. And since love is what shaped the life of Jesus, then it is love which should be the shape and focus of society, the community of Jesus, the church. Jesus said, "As the Father has loved me, so l have loved you; remain in my love."

I suppose I am somewhat a student of churches. As I have visited particular churches from time to time over many years, I have wondered not only the purpose they serve but also what shapes them, what gives them their focus and the particularities they seem to have. In studying these churches, I've discovered that some of them are shaped by some rift, some argument or disagreement which they may have suffered years ago, and which, having taken on a life of its own, shapes the lives of these churches even now.

Other churches are shaped by class or caste or color. If you are not a particular class or caste or color, you're not welcome in some churches. You can't get in. It is not always churches of the privileged that can unwelcoming. An attitude of indifference or disdain can be the character of churches of the poorer and the downtrodden as well. I have experienced this.

There are many things that can shape a church. Usually it is some quirk of history that can take a church away from the real mission of the church. But the church of Jesus Christ has but one authentic mission: to love, not in some sentimental or mushy way, but to love in substantive ways as God loved Christ and as Christ loves us. There is nothing more pathetic than a church which has forgotten that its real mission, its real business is to love. There is nothing more difficult than trying to find something praiseworthy about an irrelevant church.

The late Peter Drucker, a business management guru, told the story of an Ohio Company which at the turn of the 19th century made kerosene lamps. No question, they were good at making kerosene lamps. They were so good, in fact, that they became the world's largest purveyor of them. They were selling and shaping kerosene lamps all over the world. But, at the advent of electricity and incandescent lamps, this company still thought their business was only to make kerosene lamps. Business got slow. Eventually the company went out of business altogether. Why? Because there was no longer sufficient interest in kerosene lamps. Not many people needed or wanted what the company sold, as the electric light became king. But they would still be in business today if they understood that their ultimate mission and purpose was to provide light for as many people as possible by any good means necessary.

In like manner, the church must always be faithful to its real mission. The particulars of the mission of the church may change from time to time and place to place, but we deceive ourselves and betray our real mission unless we always and forever act upon the fact that our real mission as church is to love one another, to love the world, even as Jesus Christ has loved us.

Having said that, I'm pleased to say that there seems to be at least some love going on here at First Congregational Church here in Atlanta. I am pleased because First Church is my church and I want to be proud of it. Now you know, I have license to talk about delinquent members because I am chief among them. I send my money and promise to show up when it gets cooler. When it gets cooler, I promised to attend when it warms up at little bit. Every time Rev. Marvin Morgan comes to visit and serve communion, I promise myself and him that when I'm feeling better I'm gonna go down to the church to see if I can help out, help somebody down there. But when I feel a little better, I don't do a thing.

The point is, if First Church is like the last three churches I served, it has far too many members who are just like me. We sometimes drift into believing that the church was founded to love and to serve us. That's only half true. Christian love is a two-way street. Yes, we are loved and served by the church, but Christ calls of us to give love and to give service to others as long as we are able.

Well, I for one want to be a member in full standing in this Christian community. I hope that others will follow because if we can be fully enlisted in the community of Jesus, we are under obligation to love and serve others even as Christ loves and serves us. If we become a real part of the society of Jesus, we will love so that God can use us, and what a difference God will make in the life of the world!

In spite of my own delinquency and the delinquency of others, I am pleased to acknowledge that there is some loving going on at First Church. And, what does love looks like at First Church? We join hands and hammers with Habitat for Humanity in the building of decent housing with families who might otherwise not have access to affordable housing. That's how love looks at First Church. We partner with the Midtown Assistance Center to provide food, clothing, and counseling to those who are homeless and indigent. That's how love looks at First Church. We work with the Auburn Avenue Collaborative of Churches to meet the needs of the homeless in the Sweet Auburn area. With St. Joseph's Mercy Care Clinic, we knit scarves and gloves to provide warm clothes for those who suffer the elements in the winter. We host a support circle for persons living with HIV/AIDS. That's how love looks at First Church. We gave to our neighbors on the Gulf Coast of Mississippi and Louisiana during times of disaster and despair. We sent relief to our brothers and sisters in Haiti. Each year we collect school supplies for children in need. Our youth have hosted meals and worship with families in a shelter. That's how love looks at First Church. Our deacons help folk in need and show up at the bedsides of old folk to break the Bread of Life and to show something of the love of God. That's how love looks at First Church.

Love here at First Church looks like a group of women who organize a list of boys and girls who won't have much for Christmas unless we here at First Church give it to them. I happened to have been here the Sunday names were given. How proud I was to be given the name of a little boy. All he wanted was a big red truck. I went and bought that little boy the biggest, reddest truck I could find. He couldn't have been any more happy to receive it than I was to give it. I wish I could have been a fly on the way of the homes of all the children who received our gifts. I imagined the love of First Church and the love of Jesus come down in each of their hearts and homes. That's what love looks like at First Church.

German theologian Dietrich Bonhoeffer said years ago that Jesus was "the man for others."[1] And if Jesus was a person for others, we must be persons for others too. We are called to be Jesus people, people for others. Whatever our work or program or ministry of the moment may be, we deceive ourselves and we betray Jesus unless we know and act upon the fact that our real business, or real mission, our real purpose as a church and as Christian people is to love.

Years ago, I heard an old preacher tell a story about a church in the backwoods of Alabama where he had served as a young pastor. He said it was the custom of this little church to baptize new believers the Sunday evening after Easter. The whole church would go down to the shallow waters of a nearby river for the annual baptism. The first time he did this baptism, he walked out into the water and stood on a sand bar in the middle of the river with the candidates for baptism. The congregation gathered around a fire at the banks of the chilly river. They sang spirituals and the all-time favorite hymns of the church. They would shout and praise the Lord when each of the baptized would emerge from the water. When each candidate had been baptized they would gather with the rest of the congregation down by the riverside. The newly baptized would join in the singing and the praise.

Once everyone had been baptized, an old deacon would introduce each of the newly baptized by name and have them share what they did for a living and where they lived. When the newly baptized were done with their introductions, the deacon in charge would in turn point to each of the old members in the circle and each of them would introduce themselves and give their names. They would say something like this: "My name is Gwendolyn. If you ever get sick and need someone to wash your clothes, I'm the one. Call on me!" Or, "My name is George. If you ever need someone to chop wood for you, I'm your man. Call on me." "My name is Louise. I love children. If you ever need a place to drop off your child for a spell, my house is the place. Call on me!" "My name is Thomas. If you ever need somebody to repair your house, I've got the tools and know-how. I'm ready. Call on me!" "My name is William, I've got an old piece of a car, but I can get it started most days. If you ever need a ride to town, call on me!"

And, so it went. Once everyone was finished, the church ate a big dinner spread between the trees—a meal of fried chicken, potato salad, corn bread, black-eyed peas, collard greens—all of those wonderful black delicacies we all love to eat. When dinner was over, they would sing and shout around the campfire, praising the Lord with all that was within them. Then, when they were overcome by the chill of the night, another deacon would come up and say, "Alright folk, it's time to go." Without protest the people would leave. And, after everyone had gone, the old deacon who seemed to be in charge of everything used his big shoe to kick dirt on the fire until he knew it was out.

The preacher said in his first experience with this peculiar baptism ritual, he stayed over with the old deacon who put the fire out. He looked at the deacon and saw that he had big tears in his eyes. The tearful deacon said to the pastor, "Rev., folk don't get no closer and better than this. . . ." Then the preacher asked the deacon, "Deacon, in this church do they have a name for that ceremony you all just had?" The Deacon looked puzzled and asked, "What ceremony you talking about preacher?" The preacher said, "You know, that ceremony where each member gave their name and said what they can do to help a brother or sister out?" The deacon said, "Oh, preacher, when we go around the circle and say what we can do to help each other, we don't call that no ceremony. No, Sir, that ain't no ceremony. When we go around the circle saying how we can help each other out, we call that having church."

The preacher said from that day forward when he saw people helping each other and showing forth the love of God in Christ, he knew that was no ceremony. He knew it was having church.

My mother had been subjected to those old American Missionary Association teachers when she was growing up. Not only that, she was raised by a congregational preacher father who had gone to American Missionary Association schools from the first grade all the way through college and seminary. We used to say that Mother had been American missionized. We used to say she had been messed for sure. She had these old ways about her. For example, she believed that Sunday was holy and we had to keep it that way. We couldn't play softball, or horseshoes, or any outdoor games. We couldn't listen to jazz music, only classical. We couldn't raise our voices. We could quietly read books, especially if they were religious books, come Sunday.

I used to think what a hypocrite my mother was because at least twice a month when worship and Sunday dinner were over, she would take off her Sunday best, put on an old house dress, and go out and clean old people's houses or she would relieve those who gave care to the sick for a few hours. Or she would attend to young mothers who had just had a baby. My hypocritical mother who hardly let us breathe on Sunday would go out on Sunday to do all those things. I thought, How dare she break the Sabbath!

I was a grown man in ministry before I knew that my mother was no hypocrite. My mother wasn't breaking the Sabbath. When my mother went into those homes, she took the name of Jesus with her. She took with her the love of God. She was not breaking the Sabbath—she was having church.

You know, in my lifetime I have been a member of ten churches. I hope and pray with all my heart that First Church will be the last church I joined before I venture to that great land beyond the river and join the saints who have gone on before me. When I pass on I want to be glad I spent these last moments at old First, loving God's children and having church with you.

If I were somehow able to come back here to visit this church a thousand years from now, it is my deep prayer that First Church would not be known simply for its buildings or its prestigious members or its location or its wealth. Were I to return here a thousand years from now, I would hope that this church would be known for its love.

If I were to return even in a million years, I would hope that First Church would be having church, that it would be a loving servant church. For we are called to love each other and the world, even as God loved Christ and Christ loves us. We are commanded to abide, to continue always in Christ's love, for love is who we are. *Love is what we do.*

God of Love, help us to love one another as you have loved us.
Help us to be servants of one another
and to build up a servant church.
Amen.

Note

1. Dietrich Bonhoeffer, *Letters and Papers from Prison* (New York: Touchstone, 1953), 382.

In Memoriam

Notes on Spirituality:
A. Knighton Stanley, A Remembrance
Rev. George B. Walker Jr.

Dear family and friends, first my condolences on the loss of our dear, dear friend.

My dear sister Hope and I went to visit Doctor Stanley in June. The trip was filled with our normal banter and whooping and laughing, but it also had a somber tone that couldn't be escaped. There were serious matters to discuss, and in spite of the humorous moments, the reality of a dying man who had a sense of his journey to the land where all of us will go was a hovering presence. But because Doc was Doc, I kind of ignored just how serious he was in letting us know that he had planned for his funeral arrangements and the clarity with which he spoke. I wanted to move quickly past this part of his reality. After all, he told me that he would be my daddy. He laughed and cried regarding the recent passing of my own dad in the spring. He told me he would be there for me, and I believed that in spite of what I was seeing. I suspect that I also simply didn't want to admit that what I had so recently experienced with my own father was real. When people tell you where they are you need to believe them.

And so, here we are on this day, and my words will probably echo many. Whether you're on the dais, or sitting quietly in your chair behind the walls of this sanctuary, you will have your connections to Alfred Knighton Stanley—Tony. You will know his struggles and concerns. You will hear his laughter, his southern twang, and that special way that only he could say your name—he could say "George" like no one else. . . . But more than all of that, you will feel his spirit.

You see, dear friends, I am going to say it to you like my aunt would say to me. I am telling you something ain't nobody had to tell me about. I know this: when you're connected with folks, and truly have lived with them in good and bad, known them intimately, you have a spiritual connection that death doesn't take away. In fact, in so many ways, you—you—you—are strengthened. The Spirit will aid you in powerful ways.

When Doc told me—he didn't ask—to speak on his spirituality and the theme in general, I was taken aback. I know the spirit and I understand much about it, but to put "spirit" into words admittedly causes me a bit of unsettlement. For as confident as I could be with what I feel, to express such an obscure concept left me wanting. It's almost like describing vanilla ice cream; we can say we've tasted it, but try as we might, words fail us. But, because we are creative people we try to create an image that conjures up feelings and impulses that touch us. We hope it connects us to those around us and creates a picture we can all agree to. So let me paint a picture of what comes to mind when I think of my minister, my friend.

Picture if you will a great big banquet table. It is set in an abundant way. For vegans there will be a section with no dairy, vegetarians will have enough hummus and olive oil, our dear pesacatrians—or fish-only folks—will find wonderful pieces of snapper and tuna, along with a few pieces of catfish for good measure, the chicken eaters will have the best of rotisserie and fried options and those of us who love a good beef steak will be set. Look down the table and everything good you wanted to see will be in plain sight, but alongside all this good food and everything that is perfect will be people with whom you struggled. To quote my dear minister, "the negrorati" will be in full regalia, but this banquet also includes those who many of us wouldn't choose to be near. We would have to adjust our noses to unfamiliar smells that waif not like Tom Ford cologne or the lovely smells of Chanel, but rather the unflattering smells that have often made us cross streets or duck away. This banquet includes the least of them and the strangers, the very ones whom God calls us to love.

But here's the upshot: as God's perfected people, we would see the beauty in everyone. We would be at a place of real welcome not just tolerance. We would understand with perfect peace that each of us has been endowed with gifts unique unto us and the spiritual connection that we so sing about would be fulfilled, and in that moment we would know that we have encountered another person—really, fully, wholly.

That's a curious place and many of us don't get there. I felt so convicted by Dr. Stanley's ordination message to me because I was reminded that I, George, love a great party. Anyone who knows my spouse and me understand that we will spread a table. We love gathering the crowd. And, ironically, on this my third wedding anniversary, I am thinking much today about Dr. Stanley and his reminder to me to tend to my marriage. I think of Dr. Stanley welcoming me as a stranger and opening his table of welcome to me and expressing concretely that this is GOD's welcome table.

And I remember and honor the man who could preach one o' sermon. The first I heard in the church was with two friends with whom I am still incredibly close. The sermon came the Sunday after 9/11 and the church was quite solemn. Doc preached about the "color of God" taken in some ways from book by James McBride, *The Color of Water*. In the book the author talked about his white mother, and her journey after she left her orthodox Jewish family and married a black man. It's a story about transformation, but also about the keen observations made by a son about the purposeful life of a great mom. Doc's take was that after the terrible tragedy we suffered as a nation we would need to be mindful about how we defined what God wanted and expected. He shared incredible images that were indeed spiritual, that evoked in the congregation a sense of remembering our purpose—how do we treat the stranger, love our neighbors, and care not to judge those we do not understand? It was a powerful sermon, and in fact it was after that day I made the decision to join Peoples Church. But since I'd been to divinity school and was clear in many ways about my own path, I also knew that a great sermon wasn't going to have me join anywhere. I wanted to know what the minister thought on many subjects.

Doc and I went to lunch at a little restaurant in Georgetown a few weeks after. I told him my story and he listened and shared some of his, and assured me that I would have a home at Peoples. It was inclusive, progressive, and the Peoples people would love my gifts. I think he was right. But he also reminded me that our journey isn't an easy one. To be the church is tough work. We will endure hardships and anger, feelings of doubt and great experiences of joy. That's the spiritual side of our experience as human beings and being in shared community. That's the stuff that isn't tangible, but is felt so deeply.

When Doc said I'd talk about his spirituality, again, two things came immediately to mind: creating an open banquet table, remembering that we do not decide who God loves AND remembering his waters are indescribable. And there is a third: remembering the words that Doc often recited, and my sister Hope likes to recall, from the First Book of John, Chapter 3: "Beloved, now are we the sons and daughters of God, and it doth not yet appear what we shall be: but we know that, when he shall appear, we shall be like him; for we shall see him as he is. And every person that hath this hope in him purifieth himself, even as Christ is pure" (1 John 3:2-3, KJV, adapted). God has been mindful of us: he will bless us.

Indeed, God has been mindful of our spirits, he will bless, care for, and protect us. And with the comfort of angels he reminds that we are not alone.

Amen.

Introduction to the Funeral Sermon

Sushama Austin-Connor

I joyfully and blessedly entered ministry with the full love and support of the men who meant the most to me, most importantly, my husband, my father, my brother. And my dearest Uncle Tony. Over my high school and college years, even before seriously studying theology and enrolling at Harvard Divinity School, Uncle Tony and I spoke and wrote letters. I remember asking every (ridiculous) question under the sun — we covered relationships, homosexuality, and politics among other relevant topics. I was discovering new things and needing theological answers that only Uncle Tony could provide.

Early in my ministry, Uncle Tony and People's Church invited me to preach a woman's day service. I remember staying up for nights and all day the Saturday before I was to preach. Late in the evening Saturday, I realized that my sermon had not been saved. I will never forget my pain and embarrassment. But People's Church is home and Uncle Tony always offered comfort and safety to me. My family are still long-time members and Uncle Tony never failed to love and consider me and my gifts in his prayers and in his thinking. I preached that morning with the details of the night as my start. Uncle Tony and People's Church loved me through it, making it obvious that I was their collective child. I will never forget it. Ever.

I have too many stories to share about moments with Uncle Tony - his being formally my brother Julian's godparent and then extending that love to all of my siblings; driving to Bowling Green, KY to be with our family as we grieved our paternal grandmother's passing; our family vacations; confirming me; marrying my husband and me; baptizing my first-born; making my father laugh out loud in ways I have never seen; loving my mom through all of the crazy of family life with four children and a diva-husband; my own two boys remember his birthday party with the "Krispy Kreme donut cake" with such excitement and delight! Basically, his being a part of our lives in ways that encompassed nearly every role imaginable.

The memory, I hang on to like a lifeline is this one. I was nervous and anxious in my call, worried about my voice and worth as a future minister. I told Uncle Tony that I do not know if I have actually received a call and am concerned. With his beautiful, loving voice, he said, "Hang up. I'll call you." That meant the world to me. It still does. It is still my go-to when I worry about what this journey is truly all about.

Ministry is loving people, honoring people, and serving people. I have had no greater example of that in ministry than Uncle Tony's presence and exceptional gifts.

The greatest singular joy of my ministerial and professional life has been delivering the eulogy at his funeral service on October 10, 2013. Though it was not planned, I spoke after the iconic Rev. Jesse Jackson, Sr. If I had not already been processing into the sanctuary, I may have crawled into a hole, never to be seen again. But God! God chooses us beyond our shaky confidence, despite our fears. God chose me. Outside of my comfort zone. With my hesitant voice and what I felt was my limited oratory gifts, Uncle Tony believed in me on earth and beyond. Though I was very intimidated, I was more was so proud. I knew I had to show up. As a goddaughter. As a niece. As a parishioner. As a future colleague. And as a preacher.

12

Never Give Up

This funeral sermon, written by A. Knighton Stanley before his passing, was delivered by Sushama Austin-Connor, his God-daughter and daughter in ministry, on October 10, 2013.

> But recall those earlier days when, after you had been enlightened, you endured a hard struggle with sufferings, sometimes being publicly exposed to abuse and persecution, and sometimes being partners with those so treated. For you had compassion for those who were in prison, and you cheerfully accepted the plundering of your possessions, knowing that you yourselves possessed something better and more lasting. Do not, therefore, abandon that confidence of yours; it brings a great reward. For you need endurance, so that when you have done the will of God, you may receive what was promised. For yet
>
> "in a very little while, the one who is coming will come and will not delay; but my righteous one will live by faith. My soul takes no pleasure in anyone who shrinks back."
>
> But we are not among those who shrink back and so are lost, but among those who have faith and so are saved.
>
> (Hebrews 10:32-39)

Today, I want to preach about Christian confidence and hope. As context for our reflection, I offer you Hebrews 10:35: "Do not, therefore, abandon that confidence of yours; it brings a great reward."

Again, we read: "Do not, therefore, abandon that confidence of yours; it brings a great reward."

Frederick Buechner became one of the best-known preachers of the 20th century. In his autobiographical books about his journey into ministry,[1] Buechner speaks of his father. His father became a person of some wealth, ability, and achievement. He was outgoing and prided himself in having graduated from Princeton University. But the Great Depression had taken its toll on him, his money, and his family. He decided to throw the towel in. So, early one morning, he killed himself. A few days after his death at his own hands, his family found a cryptic note addressed to Frederick's mother on the last page of the novel *Gone with the Wind*, which he had been reading. "I adore and love you," the note said, "and am no good. ... I give you all my love."[2]

Buechner reflected on his response for many years after this tragic event. He wrote: "If ever anybody asked me how my father died, I would say heart trouble. That seemed at least a version of the truth. He had had a heart. It had been troubled."[3] Indeed, the elder Buechner's heart was troubled, very troubled.

When Frederick Buechner became a young man, he came to grips with the grief of his childhood, and he became a writer. He said of his father, "'My father seemingly felt at home everywhere,' I had one of my characters say of him. 'But he had no private home inside of himself.'"[4] So when troubles forced him home, he had no place to go—because even if he had had a home within himself, he had forgotten how to get there.

Life, however painfully, flowed on for the Buechner family, and in due season, young Frederick went off to Princeton University. Upon graduation, he was living out pretty much the same lifestyle his parents had lived. But as he grew older, there was a homesickness within him—a sickness for an inward home which his father never had.

In search of this home, he started attending the Madison Avenue Presbyterian Church in upper Manhattan. The minister at the time was the great George Buttrick, who later became pastor of the University Church at Harvard University. Dr. Buttrick was an imposing man and a great preacher. Buechner felt that when he listened to Dr. Buttrick preach and while in his presence something from beyond was breaking in upon his being.

One Sunday morning as Frederick sat listening to Dr. Buttrick, he said suddenly it was as if the Great Wall of China had come tumbling down from around his spirit. It was one of those incredible moments when God seemed to be happening in the very depths of his being and the world beyond seemed to reach in and touch the deepest place of his inner being. Frederick Buechner said it was the first time in his life that he had had a glimpse of that home and hope within his own spirit which his father never discovered. Buechner decided to enter Union Theological Seminary in New York City to study Christian Ministry.

This surprised everyone, even Frederick. One of his old family friends wondered if ministry had been his own "stupid" idea, or if he had been poorly advised. A friend from his college days wondered if he had lost his mind. Nonetheless, in spite of words of discouragement from family and friends, Buechner set out on a spiritual journey toward the Mystery which beckoned to him. Under the tutelage of the likes of Reinhold Niebuhr and Paul Tillich at Union Theological Seminary, Buechner encountered the great documents of the faith for the first time in his life.

He said in his theological studies he was initially impressed with two things: the first was that the Scriptures were earthy and honest. They were true to life. In the Scriptures, he found that there is no glossing over of the brutality and cruelty of the human story. He discovered that great heroes and sheroes of the Bible—like Abraham and Sarah, Moses and David—were flawed. Buechner was impressed by the realism and authenticity of the biblical accounts and especially the sordidness of the biblical characters. Buechner said that there was something even more astonishing than this about the biblical accounts, and that was that the worst things were never the last things in the Bible. Buechner discovered that there is a pattern in the Bible which reigns all the way from Genesis to Revelation: when human beings get to the end of their ropes, when they have borne all that they think they can bear, they discover that there is a power equal to their trust. They discover that there is a God who is able—a God who is able to take the worst things in our lives and transform them into that which is best. He learned that the God of our faith is able to take a bad situation and straighten it out and make some good of it.

When the descendants of Abraham just knew that they were on the verge of starvation, they found that Joseph, one of their own, had been brought into the king's cabinet for such a time as that and that God, through him, would supply their every need. Buechner knew that the Christian faith believes that on a Friday afternoon the best human person who ever walked the face of the earth was brutally crucified, died, and was buried. But yet, one glad Easter Sunday morning he got up, he arose from the dead. Buechner discovered that the witness of the Bible is that the worst things are never the last things. He knew that God can turn our mourning into joy. He knew at last that his father had not really died of heart trouble but of hope trouble. Frederick knew that his father hoped only in himself and not in God. He understood that his father never realized that this God of all hope always saves the very best to the very last.

Do you realize that hope is the source of the energy for your life? Do you realize that it is hope that gets us up in the morning and gets us going? If there is no hope, your life doesn't seem to go anywhere. As long as there is hope, there is life. So keep hope in your heart and walk with God.

A friend of mine accumulated a considerable amount of wealth, but he soon found himself so busy making a living that he didn't have time to make a life. He had no time to find that home, that sacred space within himself. He was so busy accumulating wealth that he had neither time to find God nor time for God to find him. When he was well-established in his business, someone sued him and he lost almost everything he had. I called him to cheer him up and to let him know he had my love and support. When I told him how sorry I was, he gave a great emotional outburst. I thought he was crying. It soon became clear to me that he was really shouting for joy.

He said to me, "When I lost almost everything I had, I became happier than I had ever been in my life." He said, "When I lost almost everything and had little left, I knew the joy of having God." One theologian said it best: "Only when I have nothing else, I know what it means to be one with God." When we trust in God the worst is never the last. The best is always in front of us. The best is yet to be.

Hebrews 10:35 speaks of maintaining hope and enduring the difficulties of life. It says, "Never throw away your confidence, never throw away your hope, because your hope, your confidence has great rewards."

Where do we get the strength to carry on in the worst of times? I'll tell you where we get it. It comes from the Christian hope and belief that there is a God, and as long as this God of hope lives, the worst things are never the last things. Even in the darkest hours this God will make a way for you. If you ask the savior to help you, God will make a way out of no way. He will carry you through.

On October 29, 1941, Winston Churchill, prime minister of Great Britain, visited Harrow School, his alma mater, and made some remarks. Included were these words: "Never give in, never give in, never, never, never, never—in nothing, great or small, large or petty—never give in except to convictions of honour and good sense."[5] Again and again in his career as a statesman, life had worked Churchill over, beaten him up, and knocked him down. On at least three occasions, his political career had been pronounced dead. But Churchill was truly the "Comeback Kid!" He was often knocked down but never out! He never gave in. He kept getting up, pressing on, and fighting the good fight. And why? Because he know what Buechner discovered in the Scriptures: that the worst things are never the last things. His heart knew the words of the old African American spiritual, "I'm so glad, trouble don't last always." He knew from the blues song of the American Negro, "everything's gonna be alright."

Churchill knew in the Christian experience of God that the best is always yet to be. Therefore, we should never give up! Never give up! Never give up! Everything's gonna be alright. Churchill was faithful even beyond the end. He planned his own funeral. At his funeral people sang great hymns, made great speeches, and prayed solemn prayers, as he had planned. And then when the benediction had been said from the altar, silence fell over the packed St. Paul's Cathedral. And just as Churchill had planned, a bugler, high in the dome of St. Paul's Cathedral, sounded the familiar notes of "Taps"— "Day is done, gone the sun," a signal that most of us recognize as marking the end of the day and the end of life. There was something about "Taps" that brought everyone a sense of the profound ending of a great life. But that was not the end. Churchill had requested that another bugler play, also high up in the dome of the cathedral, "Reveille"—"It's time to get up, it's time to get up, it's time to get up this morning!"

This final flourish of hope, which caught everyone by surprise, revealed in an instant what caused Churchill to keep on keeping on and to never give up. He never gave up because he too believed that the worst things are never the last things. The best things are always in front of us. With God, the best is always yet to be. With God, everything is gonna be alright.

It used to be when I went through the season of Lent, the crucifixion of Good Friday, and the drama of Easter, I came out of it all quite depressed. Each year I had what I came to call post-Easter depression or the post-Easter blues. I shared the fact of my post-Easter depression with an older minister friend of mine. And he said, "Son, you'll always have post-Easter depression until you remember that the crucifixion on Good Friday is not the end of Jesus. If you are going to overcome post-Easter depression you must know and believe that on the third day Jesus got up from the grave and he lives!"

I came to realize that despite this earth's cruelty and pain, God is in charge, and God always saves the best for last. When I truly came to believe that on the third day Jesus got up, Jesus rose from the dead, and that Christ lives, I had post-Easter depression no more!

Friends, I believe that because Jesus got up, because Jesus rose from the dead, the final sounds of history will not be "Taps" ("Day is done, gone the sun"). I believe that because Jesus got up, the final sounds of history will be "Reveille" ("It's time to get up, it's time to get up, it's time to get up this morning"). Why? Because there is a God. This God is with us, and this God is able. He who raised his own son from the dead—if you ask this God to help you, God is willing, God is able. God will carry you through. Never lose your confidence. Never give up hope. Hope is the best weapon against the brutality of life we could ever have in our hands and hearts. You can count on this in life and in death—joy comes in the morning. If you trust and hope in God, the worst things are never the last. If you trust in God, everything will be alright. Never give up!

Build your hopes on things eternal. Hold to God's unchanging hand!

God of Hope, Grace, and Glory,
thank you for giving us hope through the life,
death, and resurrection of your son, Jesus.
Help us to know that our hope is always in you.
Amen.

Notes

1. Frederick Buechner, *The Sacred Journey: A Memoir of Early Days* (New York: HarperCollins, 1982); *Now and Then: A Memoir of Vocation* (New York: HarperCollins, 1983); *Telling Secrets: A Memoir* (New York: HarperCollins, 1991); and *The Eyes of the Heart: A Memoir of the Lost and Found* (New York: HarperCollins, 1999). See also www.frederickbuechner.com.
2. Buechner, *The Sacred Journey*, 41.
3. Ibid., 42.
4. Buechner, *Now and Then*, 36.
5. Winston Churchill, "Never Give In, Never, Never, Never." https://www.nationalchurchillmuseum.org/never-give-in-never-never-never.html (accessed March 4, 2018).

A Memorial Poem "For Tony"

Lyvonne "Proverbs" Briggs

Breathing is the bridge between words and the heart
It is a priceless activity
To which we've grown far too accustomed
We take it for granted
Assuming that, like the sun,
Our chests will rise and set

Inhaling strength
Exhaling anxiety
Rhythmic in Spirit, much like Rev. A. Knighton Stanley

Tony was a breath of fresh air
Loving hymns
We'd sing with him
Praising the Lord
With more than a shout

But with our tears
Hot, wet, liquid salt
Trickling prayers down chiseled cheeks

And cocoa-kissed chins
Crying is worship
An encounter with God, our Creator
And Christ, our Liberator
Who beckon us to lay prostrate our egos
And, instead, risk it all
Like the ancestors who paved gravel into asphalt

Educating our babies like Mary Phillips and Mary Peake
Voting like Septima Clark, exercising our authority
There are countless foremothers who continue to inspire

My caregiver, Fannie Lou Hamer,
Who was sick and tired of being sick and tired

Organizing and encouraging like Willa B. Player

Our history is bursting if only we'd pull back the layers
Beloved, we are surrounded by a great cloud of witnesses From Martin Luther King, Jr. and Malcolm X to Andrew Young and Generation Next
Those who are here now
And those yet waiting to come forth
There is work for us to do
As we honor those who have been
We must put our hands to the plow,
"When you pray, move your feet"

A Memorial Poem for Tony

The time is now
To worship God in Spirit and in Truth
To care for the elders and nurture the youth
To speak out for the Daddy's Girl being sexually abused
To advocate for the battered woman sitting across the pew
To run bigotry and hatred right out of town
To turn this government shutdown
Upside down

This work is not easy
But God will supply our needs
Our sighs are the freedom songs of 2013
But sighs are also a sign that our breath is still moving

Liberating and loving
Lamenting and living
Praising and risking

For "We do not sail through life by clinging to the shores;
We navigate by looking at the stars."

Through his words breathed and spoken
Rev. Stanley cheers us on
So, let us unite, recite, and proclaim
That God is worthy of all our praise
Not just with our voices but all of our might

The race we must run
Evil we must fight
So that all of God's children can experience liberation
We must stand against injustice without hesitation

As Tony has slipped from time to eternity
We gained another ancestor to guide us eternally
Now, with him singing country bass in the heavenly synod
We will Praise the Lord
Risk our all
And sing little ditties about the Kingdom of God!

This poem, based on "A Call to Risk Everything for Jesus Christ" which appeared in the book, A View From My Window: 15 Sermons of Hope and Assurance, *was delivered at A. Knighton Stanley's memorial service at First Congregational United Church of Christ (Atlanta, GA) on October 6, 2013. Poet Lyvonne "Proverbs" Briggs was a recipient of the A. Knighton Stanley scholarship at Yale Divinity School.*

Afterword

Kathryn V. Stanley

Daddy was working on this book at his death. Indeed, his typist, Marjanet Wilson, delivered drafts of his handwritten pages on the eve of his death, which occurred on September 21, 2013. It has taken me more than five years to complete the project. I have been haunted by guilt for not honoring his wishes to publish this book sooner. It would be easy for me to say that the book is being released at the perfect moment, in God's perfect time, but that would ignore the human elements of procrastination on my part and the part of others, computer updates which required "finding" the typed documents once again, and all of the things that keep people from doing what they intend when they intend. Life, indeed, happens to each and every one of us. Yet our gracious God takes our failings and faltering and makes them into that which we hope honors and glorifies God.

More than five years later after Daddy's passing, life happened again. Two events have occurred that would have impacted his life significantly: the unanticipated death of his only son, my brother, Nathaniel, whom Daddy referred to as his "rock," and the birth of his first grandchild, Amari Kathryn through my sister, Taylor, and her husband, Aniefiok. The news of my brother's death and my sister's pregnancy came within days of each other. Daddy would have wept at both, grieving the loss of his son but hoping in the birth of his grandchild. At the same time, he would have grieved that he is not here to touch and feel his grandbaby, yet also rejoice that his son, his rock, has joined him after having left a legacy of compassion and faith.

With the assistance of Victoria McGoey, God has granted me a portion of strength to revisit these sermons, and even did so while reeling from the loss of my brother. While doing so, I could hear Daddy's voice and found timeless comfort in his God-inspired words. Daddy often preached sermons of hope and assurance, thus the subtitle of both this book and a previous one. Hope and assurance are always in order, for there is much in this world to be worried about, and seemingly little to find hope in, even among those of us who profess that our hope is built on Jesus. President Barack Obama is correct: Hope is an audacious enterprise. And yet, without it, without hope, we are truly doomed (as my God-son Jason used to say when he got in trouble).

And so, we grieve hard, but we hope even harder. We draw on our ancestors who hoped against hope through the Middle Passage, the degradation of slavery, and the century of domestic terrorism which followed, and even find a bit of hope in our current world where being black or brown determines one's legitimacy in spaces such as coffee shops or even one's own dormitory lounge, and where the knee of white supremacy remains on our necks. We draw on the life-giving words of a father, who has joined the great cloud of witnesses whose rest has already been won. Because of them, we win no matter what.

About the Author

Alfred Knighton (Tony) Stanley was born on July 15, 1937 in Dudley, North Carolina. He was the youngest of five children of the Rev. Joseph Taylor Stanley and Kathryn Turrentine Stanley. It was in tiny Dudley at First Congregational Church and in the loving arms of his older sister, Joye, that he first experienced God's presence. It was in the loving arms of Joye's son, Victor McLean, that he entered into God's eternal presence on September 21, 2013 in Atlanta, Georgia.

In June 1964, Rev. Dr. Stanley married Beatrice Alice Perry, whom he had met during his summer internship at Central Congregational United Church of Christ in New Orleans. They were the parents of Nathaniel Taylor Stanley and Kathryn Velma Stanley. In 1986, Dr. Stanley was married to Andrea J. Young, and they were the parents of Taylor Marie Stanley. Dr. Stanley had an undying love for and an interest in children, and he was fond of saying of his children: "Taylor is my joy, Kathie is my heart, and Nathaniel is my rock."

Dr. Stanley was a graduate of Talladega College, Alabama, and earned a Master's Degree from Yale Divinity School and a Doctorate from Howard University. Upon graduation from

Yale in 1962, he became Director of the Southern Christian Fellowship Foundation at North Carolina Agricultural and Technical University, and in 1964 he joined the faculty and administration of Bennett College. In both of these positions he was active in the 1963 phase of the Greensboro, North Carolina, Civil Rights Movement. He served as advisor to the local chapter of the Congress of Racial Equality and was appointed to the Human Rights Commission of the City of Greensboro. He emerged as a principal strategist in the all-important sit-in campaign there against Jim Crow laws.

Dr. Stanley served as Associate Pastor of Plymouth Congregational United Church of Christ in Detroit, Michigan, from 1966–1968. From 1968–2006 he served as Senior Minister of Peoples Congregational United Church of Christ in Washington, D.C. During that time it was Dr. Stanley's skillful and thoughtful preaching that grew the congregation and built a culturally inspired new sanctuary and dynamic ministries for young and old alike. Peoples Church became home to a daycare center, a community credit union, and D.C.'s largest Boy Scout and Girl Scout programs. It expanded a scholarship program that still recognizes church and community graduates from pre-school to Ph.D. Classic Negro spirituals, urban gospel, and jazz became common musical fare, along with sermons of national leaders and Dr. Stanley's own, in which he characteristically blended biblical teachings with folk wisdom and current events in a manner that nurtured Christian souls.

The collection of sermons in Dr. Stanley's second book, *A View from My Window: 15 Sermons of Hope & Assurance*

About the Author

(Fideli Publishing, 2008), provides a glimpse of the food for the spirit and mind that was served at Peoples each Sunday for thirty-eight years. Dr. Stanley's first book, *The Children Is Crying: Congregationalism Among Black People* (Pilgrim Press, 1978), was his doctoral thesis.

Dr. Stanley served his denomination in numerous capacities. He was a member of the Committee on Theological Education; a member of the Council for Christian Social Action; President of Ministers for Racial and Social Justice; and a member of the Board of the Office of Communications. He served as a member of the New Century Hymnal Committee; a member of the Nominating Committee of the General Synod; a member of the Large Gifts Committee of the Denomination's Capital Funds Campaign; and as a consultant for the revision of the Book of Worship for the United Church of Christ. He served on the Church in Ministry Committee of the Potomac Association and as a member of the Board of Directors of the Central Atlantic Conference of the United Church of Christ. Dr. Stanley was Chair of the Board of Ministers Life Insurance Company, which is now a part of Minnesota Life. He was founding President of the Collaboration of African American Men and Boys, a program of the Kellogg Foundation. He was a member of the Board of Advisors of the Yale University Divinity School. Dr. Stanley was the writer of many articles and was former publisher of The New American Missionary. He traveled extensively to Asia, Africa, the Caribbean, and the Middle East.

Dr. Stanley distinguished himself in many capacities. During the Bicentennial era, he served as Executive Director of the Office of Bicentennial Programs of the Nation's Capital and Special Assistant to Walter E. Washington, then-mayor of the District of Columbia. He served as Chair of the Board of Trustees of the University of the District of Columbia and as a member of the Advisory Board of Industrial Bank of Washington, and served on the Judiciary Nominating Committee for the Superior Court and the Court of Appeals of the District of Columbia. He was the founder and General Secretary of the Petworth Assembly and a member of the Board of Directors of the National Interfaith Alliance. He was Founding President of the Faith Based Community Action Partnership.

After retiring from Peoples, Dr. Stanley was minister for Church Development at St. Albans Congregational Church/United Church of Christ, in St. Albans (Queens), New York. He then relocated to Atlanta, where he was a member of First Congregational UCC in Atlanta, Georgia. In Atlanta his ministry continued through Facebook and weekly handwritten notes to family and friends.

www.ingramcontent.com/pod-product-compliance
Lightning Source LLC
Chambersburg PA
CBHW072019110526
44592CB00012B/1376